D1326491

200 Boredom Busters!

A DORLING KINDERSLEY BOOK
www.dk.com

For my son, Alistair

Senior Editor Lee Simmons
Art Editor Mandy Earey
Additional Design Jacqui Burton
Managing Editor Mary Ling
Managing Art Editor Rachael Foster

Photography Steve Gorton
Production Lisa Moss
DTP Designer Almudena Díaz
Picture Research Sally Hamilton,
Neale Chamberlain, Lee Thompson

First published in Great Britain in 1999 by
Dorling Kindersley Limited
9 Henrietta Street, London, WC2E 8PS
2 4 6 8 10 9 7 5 3 1

Copyright © 1999 Dorling Kindersley Limited

All rights reserved. No part of this publication
may be reproduced, stored in a retrieval
system, or transmitted in any form or by any
means, electronic, mechanical, photocopying,
recording, or otherwise, without the prior
written permission of the copyright owner.

A CIP catalogue record for this book is
available from the British Library.

ISBN: 07513 5891 6

Colour reproduction by Colourscan, Singapore
Printed and bound in Italy by L.E.G.O.

About Boredom Busters

"I'm bored." How often have you said that? You've got the whole day ahead of you and nothing to do. Well, let Boredom Busters come to the **rescue!** There are so many exciting ideas in this book, you'll **never** be bored again.

200 Boredom Busters is divided into themes, which will take you from making obstacle courses to **exploring** in the jungle, and much more. Watch out for these symbols as you go. **Did you know ?** will tell you an interesting fact connected to the theme you are working on. **A bright idea** is yet another project for when you're at a loose end. The **warning sign** ⚠ indicates that extra care is needed – ask an adult to help you. Play safe and have lots of fun with these Boredom Busters!

200 Boredom Busters!

Paul Scott

A DORLING KINDERSLEY BOOK
London • New York • Moscow • Sydney
www.dk.com

Contents

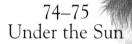

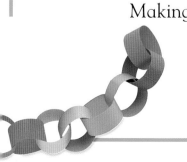

Indoor antics

There's nothing to do. Even being at school would be more fun. **Invite** your **friends** to **try** out these **games**.

You will need
- 2 sheets of card
- 16 split pins
- Insulated wire
- 4.5V battery
- 3.5V bulb
- Bulb holder
- 2 paper-clips

Matching pairs quiz

Impress your friends with this electrical circuit board game.

1 Turn a piece of card sideways. Divide it into four equal columns, then cut out two columns of eight "windows"; one each side of the centre. Fold the outer columns into the centre to make flaps. Fix a split pin next to each window.

2 Turn the card over and number the split pins on the left one to eight. Then number the split pins on the right, but jumble up the number order. Use short lengths of insulated wire to join the two "ones", the two "twos", and so on.

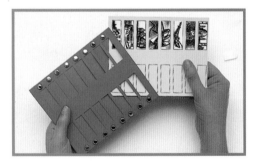

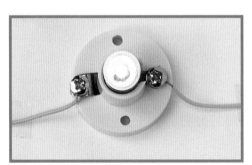

3 Cut the second piece of card so it slides into the quiz board, then draw the window areas on to the card. Pick a topic with well-known pairings, then remembering how the windows are linked, write or draw in the pairs.

4 To make the tester, take three pieces of wire. Attach one to a battery terminal, one from the other battery terminal to the bulb holder, and one to the free side of the bulb holder. Attach a paper-clip to the two free ends.

Make a word-pairing or a picture-pairing game . . . or even a picture and word-pairing game!

The fancy fish race

Make some tissue-paper fish. Now flap a rolled-up newspaper behind the fish and float them across the floor. Who will win?

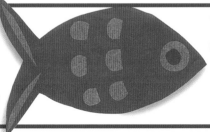

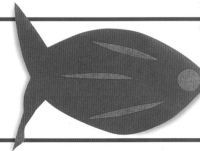

Try other pairings, such as countries and their capital cities or football teams and their captains or goalkeepers.

Badminton ●

Cricket ●

Tennis ●

Golf ●

American football ●

Table tennis ●

Baseball ●

Football ●

Hands up!

To play this game you need a small coin and two teams sitting opposite each other at a table. Team A takes the coin first. They pass it under the table and one member hides it in his or her hand. Team B's leader then gives the order "Hands up!". Team A place their clenched hands on the table. Then Team B's leader tells them to do one of three things:

Creepy Crawly: Move fingers forward in a crawling motion.

Wibbly Wobbly: Clench your hands and turn them over and back.

Flat Out: Lay your hands flat on the table.

Team B must guess who is holding the coin. A correct guess means it is Team B's turn. If wrong, Team A has another turn.

5 Now you're ready to play! All your friends have to do is to match the correct pairs together. To check they are right, get them to place the paper-clips on the two fasteners beside their choices. A correct answer will light up the bulb!

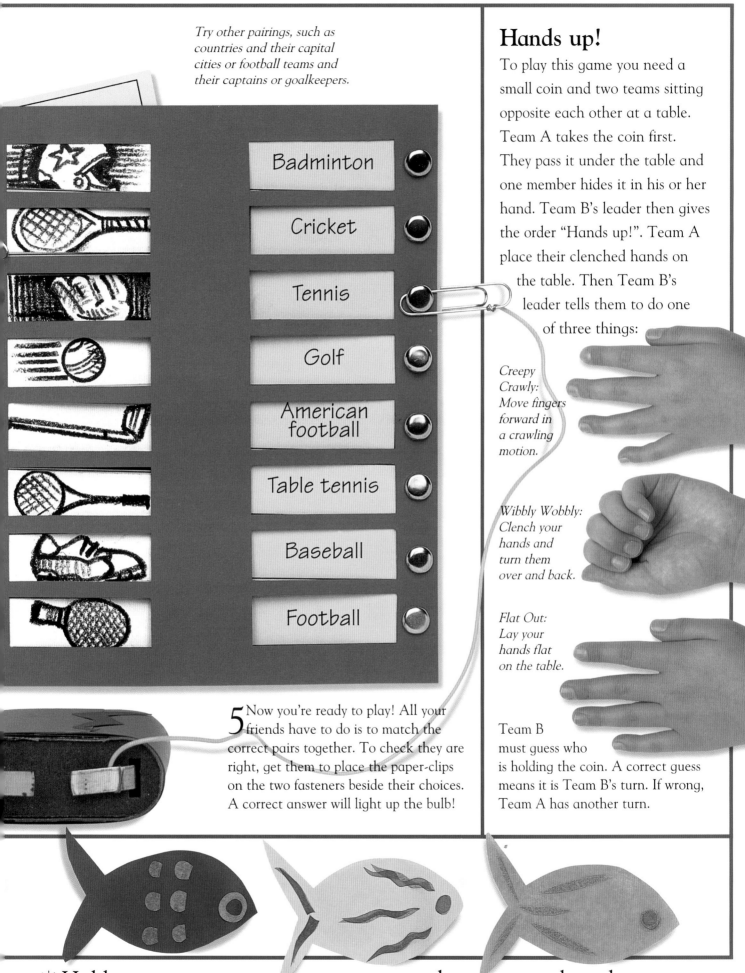

☀ Hold a "board" evening! Invite your friends round and play your favourite board games.

What a waste!

Sometimes we **throw out** things without thinking that they could be **recycled** or perhaps be of **use** to someone else. However, did you know that you can have a lot of **fun** with empty bottles, waste paper, and packaging?

Avoid putting cooked food or fat in your compost as it will attract rats.

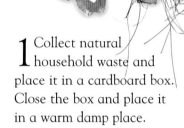

Make a bottle band

Using clean glass bottles, add differing amounts of water to each, as shown. Now strike each one gently with a stick. Can you play a tune?

Change the sound the bottle makes by altering the amount of water it contains. Try using a musical instrument to tune your bottles to particular notes.

1 Collect natural household waste and place it in a cardboard box. Close the box and place it in a warm damp place.

Cast-off collage

Collect lots of different types of clean waste material, such as paper, card, plastic, paper-clips, and rubber bands. Use them to make a great-looking picture, which you can then frame and hang in your room.

1 On a sheet of card, draw your picture outline, keeping the shapes fairly simple. Cut out pieces from your waste to fill the shapes.

2 Glue the background pieces in place first, then build up your picture by adding more layers. When the glue is dry, add paint.

3 Allow the paint to dry before colouring in details such as clouds. Complete your work of art with a frame.

Choose materials with texture to give life to your picture. Corrugated card, used edge on, is good for buildings.

Make a **wastepaper** basket out of cardboard covered in **papier mâché** (see pages 34–35).

Don't waste your waste!

Did you know you can recycle such items as vegetable peelings, dead flowers, rotten fruit, or grass cuttings. Make a compost heap and turn this waste into a perfect fertilizer for plants.

2 Continue adding waste to your box until it is full and then leave it. After one or two months, the compost should be ready to use!

Your compost will make a very nutritional meal for your plants!

A–Z scavenger hunt

In this game you and your friends divide into teams of two or three. Each team writes the alphabet, in order, down the side of a sheet of paper. Then, you have 30 minutes to collect waste objects from around your home or garden. You need to collect one object for each letter of the alphabet. The objects must fit into a carrier bag and should be recorded on the team sheet. The winners are the team who have collected the most objects.

The objects should be things that would otherwise have been thrown away or discarded, such as drinks cans, packaging, fallen twigs, or flower seeds.

Poster power

Large, colourful posters are a great way to put a message across to others. Design a poster to remind people not to be wasteful. Here are a couple of ideas to start you thinking.

Give your poster a professional look by producing it on a computer.

Contact your local authority about their recycling policy.

And there's more . . .

Recycle it

Decorate three large cardboard boxes to collect waste paper, cans, and glass. Find out where your nearest recycling depot is and empty the boxes out each week.

Money for waste

Some charities collect stamps or aluminium drinks cans, which they sell to raise money. Contact local charities and ask if they could use your stamps or cans.

Eggy mosaics

You can make an unusual mosaic with broken egg shells. Draw a design onto card. Then paint the shells, crush them into smaller pieces, and glue them down.

Use discarded **packaging** to create an **alien** monster.

Holiday fun

You're on holiday! Grab a camera, scrapbook, and coloured pencils and enjoy these great ideas.

Pack your suitcase!

Pass the time with this suitcase game. Player 1 starts the game by saying, for example, "I'm going on

holiday and I'm packing sunglasses."

Player 2 repeats the first item and then adds their own saying, "I'm going on holiday and I'm packing sunglasses and . . . ."

At each turn, players have

to list all the items that have gone

before, in the correct order, plus add one more item to the list. Any mistakes and you are out of the game!

How much can you and your friends pack into the suitcase?!

Holiday scrapbook

Keep a diary of what you do each day of your holiday. A diary doesn't have to be just a written account. You can also include your own pictures and photographs.

My Summer Holiday

Friday 7th August   We had to be at the airport really early. We ate breakfast in the airport café.

Saturday 8th August   We went cycling in the countryside and had a picnic in a field of cows!

Draw pictures of your favourite trips.

Write the date and a brief description under each item to bring those memories flooding back!

☆ Think of an object. Can your friend guess it in twenty guesses? You can only answer yes or no!

Add things you have collected, such as postcards, stamps, coins, tickets, and other souvenirs.

Monday
10th August

Went on a boat trip in the morning.

Later we played with friends on the beach.

Fantastic photos

A camera is a great way to record people and places. Try these different techniques to create really unusual pictures.

Starburst

Dab petroleum jelly onto some cellophane and wipe it in a diagonal direction with a tissue, pressing down hard. Repeat on the reverse, wiping in the opposite direction to form "X" shapes. Tape it to your lens when taking a night-time picture of bright lights to create a starburst effect.

Colour filters

Make coloured filters with cellophane sweet wrappers. Tape a wrapper over your camera lens to tint your picture. To make a two-colour picture, tape two wrappers together, and stick them over your lens in the same way.

Pebble painting

Collect a selection of pebbles. Wash and dry them thoroughly. Decorate them with colourful painted designs or pictures. Leave to dry, then add a coat of varnish.

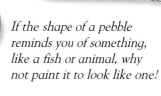

Happy memories

When you come home again, your diary will remind you of all the fun you had; where you went, who you met, and what you did!

If the shape of a pebble reminds you of something, like a fish or animal, why not paint it to look like one!

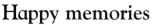

Pen and paper

There are many types of **paper:** writing paper, wrapping paper, newspaper, wallpaper. All of these **projects** make use of paper or **card** which you will have at home.

Handmade paper

Here's one way to make your very own handmade paper from throwaway scraps of used paper, and a few ideas for using it.

1 Tear up lots of paper into small pieces and place them in a bowl. Fill two-thirds of the bowl with water and whisk until the paper becomes a pulp. Alternatively, you can whizz it in a blender for about 30 seconds.

2 Pour the pulp into a large tray or dish, add some more water, and stir well. Slip a piece of fine wire mesh into the pulp. Let a layer of pulp settle on top of the mesh, then carefully lift the mesh out and leave it to drain.

3 Lay the mesh on some newspaper and place a dry, absorbent cloth on top. Turn the pile upside-down, and press on the newspaper to help it absorb excess water. Carefully lift up the newspaper and mesh. Allow the paper to dry out.

Experiment by using different types of paper or by adding petals or glitter.

4 Use your handmade paper to write someone a letter, make a card, paint a picture, or even just frame it!

If your paper curls at the edges, weigh it down with books to flatten it.

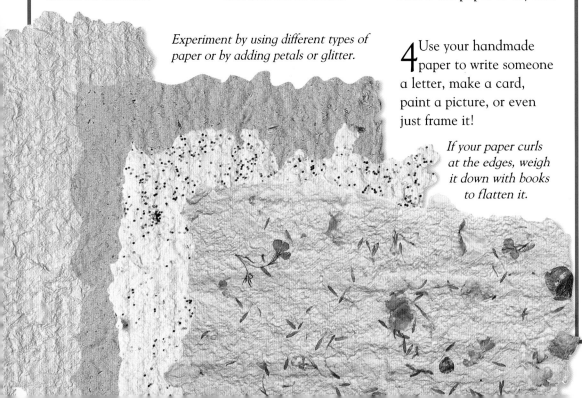

Pop-up surprise

Is someone you know having a birthday? Surpris them with a pop-up card.

1 Fold a piece of card in half then open it. Draw your picture so that half of it is above the fold. Cut around the half above the fold, as shown.

Springy snakes

Here is a great idea for a pop-up card that will give your friends a real shock when they open it. Watch their faces and have a laugh!

1 Fold a sheet of card in half to form the main part of your pop-up card. Next, take some coloured card and draw the outline of a coiled-up snake. Cut it out, as shown.

2 Fold the card in half and it should stand without the need of further support.

And there's more . . .

Pictorial typeface

Design a decorative typeface. Combine letters and shapes, such as a letter "S" in the shape of a snake. Use your new alphabet to make a great-looking nameplate for the door of your room.

Bamboo pen

Shape the end of a piece of bamboo to make a pointed nib shape. Dip into ink and write!

Hieroglyphs

A picture which represents a word or an object is called a hieroglyph. For example, an eye represents the word "see". Make up your own hieroglyphs and write in code to a friend.

Treasure island map

Tear the edges of a piece of paper, soak it in cold tea, then leave it to dry. When almost dry, sprinkle a few granules of coffee over the surface. When dry, shake off the granules and you have a sheet of ancient-looking paper! Draw a map of an island and label it with pirate-sounding names, such as Treasure Beach and Shiver-Me-Timbers Forest. Mark hidden treasure with an "X".

2 Decorate your snake using pens and pieces of coloured paper. Colour the inside of the card to look like long grass in the jungle. Glue the end of the snake's tail to the right side of the card and stick the head on the left, and wait for it to spring a surprise!

Make **paper planes** with your friends and see whose plane flies the furthest.

Sound and music

Do you enjoy listening to music? Maybe you play an instrument yourself. It can also be good fun to experiment with different sound effects – why not have a go!

Rattling rhythms

Collect as many metal bottle caps as you can. Decorate a stick or pole with paint and coloured tape. Ask an adult to help you loosely nail the caps to it with several caps on each nail. Tap your "zob stick" on the ground for a really rhythmic sound! !

Give it a shake

Pour a cup of rice or dried beans into two empty plastic bottles that you have decorated. Attach sticks to the bottles with tape and there you have it – easy shakers!

Decorate the bottles with acrylic paint, or poster paint mixed with PVA glue.

Knock coconut shells together to sound like galloping horses.

Radio stories

When you listen to a story on the radio, you'll hear sound effects that are added in the studio to make the story more real. Write and record a story onto tape using different characters and sound effects.

Strum it!

Here is a quick and easy way to make a simple guitar. Take a small box, such as a shoe box, and cut a circle out of the lid. Fold the circle, as shown, and glue it in place to form the bridge of the guitar. Insert six split pins at each end of the box, and stretch six elastic bands between the pins and over the bridge. Make sure the strings are tight and away you go – pluck the strings and make music!

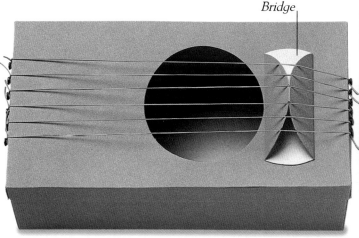

Bridge

Stretch the bands tighter for a higher pitch.

Why not paint your guitar in a rockstar style?

Form a band with your friends.

Rub a shoe on to stones to sound like a person walking.

Pop a balloon with a pin to sound like a car backfiring.

Try recording your story just using the sound effects. Can your friends work out what is happening?!

Sound it out

Read through your story and think about the sounds you want to add, then decide how you will create them. Wobble a piece of card for thunder, sprinkle water from a watering can for rain, blow bubbles into water with a straw for a bubbling cauldron. There are endless ideas!

Musical grass

Who would have thought that a blade of grass could create a sound! Find a thick piece of grass and stretch it tightly between your thumb tips and thumb bases as shown below. Blow through the gap between your thumbs and the grass should shriek!

And there's more . . .

Hose horn

Make a horn by attaching a funnel to the end of a length of hose pipe. Purse your lips tightly, press them against the end of the tube, and blow hard. Beware – it may take a little practice!

Name that tune!

Hum short sections of well-known songs. Can your friends guess what they are?

Keep in time

Sing along to a song on a tape or CD. Turn the sound down suddenly, but carry on singing. After about 15–20 seconds, turn the sound back up. Are you at the same point in the song as the tape? Try it with a friend!

The shorter the piece of hose the better, but ask the owner first before you cut it!

Host a sound quiz with a tape of household noises.

Picture perfect

Would you like to be an artist? Experiment with these ideas to **create** your own masterpieces. They may not be as valuable as a Picasso or van Gogh, but they will **make** beautiful **decorations**.

Magazine close-ups

Make some amazing close-up pictures. All you need is a pile of old magazines and a simple close-up frame, such as the one shown here.

1 To make your close-up frame, draw a 10-cm square onto card. Draw a 7-cm square inside the first, then cut it out.

2 Next, look through some old magazines and use your close-up frame to pick out interesting details in larger pictures.

Incredible ink-blowing

Ink-blowing is fun – and you can make great pictures too! Brush watered-down paint across a piece of paper to make the background. Drop blobs of ink onto the page. Using a straw, blow the ink in different directions to create a weird and wonderful landscape.

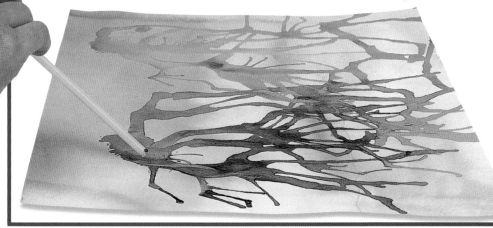

Ink-blot monsters

Make ink-blot monsters to add to your scene. Fold a piece of paper in half. Open it and place a drop of ink or paint in the fold. Fold again and press firmly. Reopen it up and leave to dry.

Flick through an **art book**. Choose your favourite painting. What can you find out about the artist?

3 Once you have selected your favourite close-up, make a frame out of card. Stick your picture to the back of the frame.

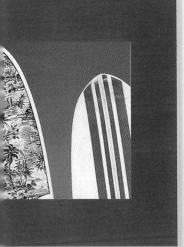

You can use any type of card to make the frame, as long as it is not too thin. Try corrugated cardboard or coloured paper.

You could also decorate your frame with simple images.

Traffic madness

Display snaps of your friends and family in this novel-looking frame. Draw a picture of a vehicle such as a bus, car, or aeroplane, keeping the shape simple and making sure the windows are large enough to stick a photograph in. Cut the window holes out and place a photograph behind each window.

You may need to cut some photographs to fit. Make sure you have permission to do this first!

Scratch it!

Using wax crayons, completely cover a sheet of paper in a random pattern of colours. Then paint over the wax with black paint. When dry, scrape a picture or design using forks, spoons, or other kitchen utensils.

You can frame your finished picture and hang it in your bedroom.

Kitchen magic

Balancing tightrope walkers, **erupting** volcanoes . . . and you thought the kitchen was just somewhere to do the **washing up**!

You will need

For the biscuits
- 275 g plain flour
- 1 teaspoon baking powder
- 75 g butter
- 100 g soft brown sugar
- 1 small egg
- 50 g golden syrup

For the icing
- 100 g icing sugar
- 1 tablespoon of hot water

For the chocolate icing
- 75 g icing sugar
- 25 g cocoa powder
- 1 tablespoon hot water

Biscuit bonanza

These biscuits are fun to make, quick to cook, and yummy to eat! Set the oven to 170°C/325°F/Gas Mark 3 before you start.

Remember to ask permission before you use the kitchen!

1 Sift the flour and baking powder into a bowl. Cut the butter into small pieces, and add to the mixture with the sugar. Rub the mixture between your fingertips until it looks like breadcrumbs.

2 Break the egg into a jug and beat with a fork. Mix in the syrup. Make a hollow in the flour mixture and add the egg mixture. Beat until it becomes a ball of dough.

3 Chill the dough in the fridge for 30 minutes. Roll it out to 0.5 cm thick and cut out your favourite shapes. Place on a baking tray and bake for 15–20 minutes. Leave to cool.

4 To make the icing, sift the icing sugar into a bowl and add water until you have a smooth paste. For chocolate icing, mix the icing sugar with cocoa powder before adding water.

5 Spread the icing on the biscuits and you're ready to decorate! Use cherries or a sprinkling of icing sugar.

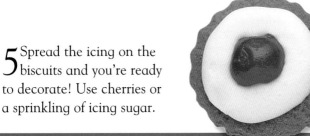

Magic egg

Challenge your friends to balance an egg on its end. With a little know-how, it's easy!

This trick also works well with sugar.

1 Make a small pile of salt. Place the egg in the centre. Now very gently, blow the salt away.

2 Once the pile of salt has gone, the egg will look as if it is balancing on it's end! Your friends will have to look very closely to see that the egg is really sitting on a few tiny grains of salt.

Can you make an **egg** bounce? Hardboil an egg then soak it in vinegar for a week. Now bounce it!

Tightrope walker

Try this fascinating balancing act and amaze your friends. Draw a picture, such as a colourful bird or a boat on the high seas, on to a piece of thin card.

1 Push two forks into a cork, as shown, tilting the forks forwards and down. Make a notch in the end of a matchstick. Push the match head into the cork base.

2 Now cut out the image you have drawn and stick it to the cork with sticky tape, making sure the end of the matchstick just sticks out below the picture.

3 Create a tightrope with a piece of string and balance the matchstick on it. It's tricky, but it can be done! Make sure the string is pulled tight.

If the picture doesn't balance straight away, adjust the forks slightly.

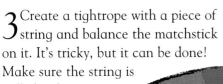

And there's more . . .

Juicy jewellery!

These unusual necklaces and bracelets make excellent gifts. Thread dried melon seeds or fruit on to nylon thread. In fact, you can use any sort of food, but make sure it has been dried first! Add paint to the melon seeds for a bit of colour.

Erupting volcano

Half fill a bottle with bicarbonate of soda and place in a dish. Pile gravel, then sand around the bottle to make the volcano. Colour some vinegar with red food colouring. Pour it quickly into the bottle and stand by for the eruption!

Fun of the fair

Organize your very own funfair in the back garden. Here are ideas for lots of really exciting games that you could make. Invite your friends to join in the fun!

Walking tall

You will be walking tall when you use these stilts! They have two sets of steps, so you can make them easier or more difficult to use. The stilts are made from wood, which needs to be cut to size – ask an adult to do this for you or get them cut at the timber merchants. **!**

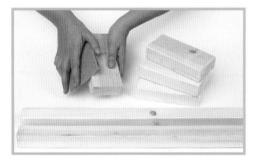

1 Take the two 150-cm pieces of wood and the four 15-cm blocks of wood and smooth the edges with sandpaper. The short blocks will be the steps and the long pieces will be the stilts.

2 Glue a step to the inside of one of the long pieces of wood, 25 cm from the end. Clamp the step until the glue is dry. Glue the second step to the outside edge of the wood, 50 cm from the same end.

You will need
• Two 150 x 3 x 3 cm pieces of wood
• Four 15 x 7 x 3 cm blocks of wood
• Wood glue
• Acrylic paints

Start on the lower set of steps. Find a soft surface such as grass to practise on – just in case you fall off!

3 Glue the remaining two steps to the other length of wood in the same way. Paint your stilts with colourful patterns and when the paint is dry, practise walking on them.

Make your own hoopla game by throwing home-made wire hoops over sticks stuck in the ground.

Knock-down cans

You and your friends will love this great fairground game. You will need 10 used tin cans, all the same size. Cover the cans with coloured paper, then stack them up in a pyramid shape. Now find four small balls, and you are ready to play! Players take it in turns to throw the balls at the cans. The winner is the person who knocks over the most cans.

If you don't have coloured paper to decorate your cans, use ordinary paper and paint them with poster or acrylic paint.

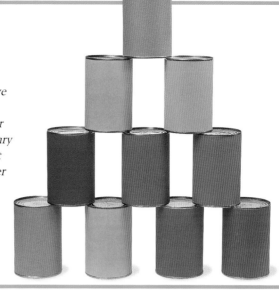

Apple tree challenge

Draw the outline of a tree with branches and some large apples on a big piece of thick card. Cut out the tree, then cut around the outline of each apple making each apple bigger than your ball. Paint your tree with poster paint and prop it up securely with some large stones. The challenge is to throw a ball through the apple-shaped holes. Award a different score for each hole. Now hand out the balls, and take turns to throw!

You can use balls or beanbags.

Clowning around

Clowns make people happy. Paint a clown face and get all your friends to join in and create their own designs.

3 Using a fine brush, add colourful patterns and glitter to your face. All you need now is a crazy hat!

1 Using face paints, sponge three stripes of colour across your face. Then paint the tip of your nose and your lips pink.

2 Paint a triangle over one eyebrow and a rainbow over the other. Add pink diamonds round your eyes.

Twist and **wrap** elastic bands into a huge, bouncy ball!

Backyard nature

Sometimes the backyard can seem very still and quiet and maybe a little boring. But look a little closer and listen a little harder and you'll find creatures and interesting plants everywhere!

Tie string around the top of your pine cone. Hang both your feeders on a tree branch.

Leaf library

Leaves come in all sorts of shapes and sizes. Make a collection of them and stick them into a scrapbook. Can you identify the plants or trees your leaves came from? A book about trees may come in useful.

See how many different leaf shapes you can collect.

Leafy prints

You can make some fantastic pictures by taking prints of leaf shapes and vein patterns. Be creative and use lots of different colours. Brush your leaf with a light coating of paint. Press a sheet of paper on top of the painted surface, then peel it off carefully.

Keep the paper very still when it is on the leaf.

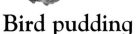

Bird pudding

During the cold winter months, feed the birds with this tasty treat. Mix together breadcrumbs, cheese, porridge oats, and birdseed. Add soft cooking fat, then push into the gaps of a pine cone before it sets.

Nutty delight

Thread peanuts in their shells and other nuts on to string for small birds to hang on.

Bug traps

To identify the insects and small animals in your garden, you need to catch them first. Make these traps, observe them and then let them go.

Insect hideaway

Sink a yoghurt pot into a small hole in the ground. Add some bait, such as a piece of bacon rind. Place a tile, supported on four stones, over the pot.

Minibeast trap

Cut a grapefruit in half and scoop out the middle. Put cubes of bread in it and place it in a sheltered spot in the garden.

Check your traps regularly. Does different food attract different insects?

Some insects are dangerous, so observe without touching them.

Snail trails

Have fun keeping track of the snails in your garden. You will be surprised how many snails you will see! Keep a snail log book to record your findings!

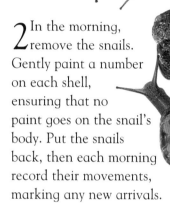

1 Put a large flowerpot on its side outside. The snails will climb in.

2 In the morning, remove the snails. Gently paint a number on each shell, ensuring that no paint goes on the snail's body. Put the snails back, then each morning record their movements, marking any new arrivals.

And there's more . . .

Bark rubbings

Place a sheet of paper on the bark of a tree and rub over it with a crayon. Take rubbings from a variety of trees using different coloured crayons to make a beautiful bark collection.

Spore prints

Place a shop-bought mushroom cap, gill-side down, onto coloured card. Put a bowl over it and leave. The next day, carefully lift the cap off the card. The spores should have made a print!

Keep a **record** of all the different creatures that **visit** your garden in one afternoon.

Ready, steady, GO!

Here's a great idea for an outdoor obstacle course, which you and your friends can have fun building. Challenge each other, using a stopwatch, to see who can go round in the fastest time!

3 Now walk along the plank. Try not to fall off! If you do, you'll have to start again!

2 Carefully dribble a ball in and out of a line of upturned buckets. Take it slowly, as it requires good ball control!

4 Jump into the balloon pool and find the hidden boiled egg. Add time penalties for bursting a balloon or cracking the egg! Take the egg with you to the end of the course.

8 Put down the egg and spoon. Jump or climb over the pole, and stop the watch!

FINISH

START

1 Go! Start by doing a limbo under the pole. Remember to start the timer!

☀ Meet your friends at the **park** for an afternoon of games.

5 As fast as you can, crawl under a blanket held down along the sides with stones.

Too easy?
After timing each person with a stopwatch, make the course even more of a challenge. Try it with your legs tied together at the knees!

6 Wriggle your way through an old tyre. Hold on to that egg!

You can vary the obstacles you use depending on what you can find in your home.

7 Pick up a spoon to carry your egg to the finish. Step in and out of the ladder rungs one by one. No cheating by trying to miss some out!

And there's more . . .

Blowing bubbles
Mix a solution of one tablespoon of washing-up liquid, one tablespoon of glycerine, and a cup of cold water. Make a loop from a piece of thick wire. Dip the loop into the solution and gently blow bubbles as big as you can!

Bat and ball
One person has a bat, a racket, or even a piece of wood! The others spread out in a circle and try to throw a ball at the batter's legs. The batter must try to hit the ball before it touches them. They can't move their feet but can twist around. If someone hits their legs or catches the ball before it bounces, they become the batter. The ball must be thrown from wherever it lands.

Quick jacks
Scatter five jacks, or pebbles, on the ground. Throw one up then pick up another before catching the first. Repeat until you have lifted all the jacks.

Sack race
Here is a game that even the fastest runner will find tricky! Each person climbs into a sack or pillowcase. Then race each other by jumping to the finish line.

Relay race
Run relay races with two or more teams, each consisting of three or four runners. The first runner runs to a turning point and back, then the second runner does the same, and so on. Try different races where runners have to hop, jump, or even run backwards!

If you enjoy the **outdoors**, find out about **orienteering** – it's a great sport!

Curtain up!

Performing a play in front of your friends and family can be really exciting. You can still manage it, even if you don't have a real theatre in which to act. Make your own mini-theatre, complete with scenery and characters!

Building a theatre

First, decide on a story and plot. For example, you could perform a story about little people in a land of giants, and the adventures they have. Write it down, scene by scene. Next you need to design and build your theatre and scenery and make the "actors".

You will need
- Cardboard box
- Coloured paper
- Glue
- Old magazines
- Card
- Old photographs

Invite some friends or family members to join in the fun – building the theatre, reading the story, or moving the characters.

1 Take a cardboard box and remove the top flaps. Glue coloured paper to the inside and outside of the box. When dry, cut away part of the sides, as shown.

Ask someone to do the sound effects for you. You'll find some ideas on pages 14–15.

2 Cut out magazine pictures of grass and stick them to the theatre floor. Next, cut grass shapes out of green paper, as shown, and glue these to the inside walls and around the outside edge of the theatre.

3 For the scenery, cut out objects from magazines. Glue on to card and draw a flap at the base of the cards, as shown. Cut out the objects and flaps, then fold the flaps back to make the objects stand up.

4 To make the actors, look through old photographs and magazines for pictures of people. Select some large animal pictures too. Glue them to a sheet of card, then cut them out when they are dry.

Learn a funny story or poem to recite as a party piece.

Choose a date for the opening night of your play and design a poster to advertise it.

Place your poster where everyone will see it and make invitations to send to your friends and family.

As a nice, finishing touch to your production, provide some refreshments for your guests.

Use the long handles to move your figures in and out of the action.

5 Ask an adult to help you cut a slit along the top and down one side of the box, as shown. Make sure it is big enough to slot in your giant animal, as this is where it will make its grand entrance.

6 Make stands for your cut-out people with card. Make a single slit in the feet. Cut out a small rectangle of card and make a slit in both sides, as shown. Slot the cut-out person's feet into one slit and fit a long, thin strip of card (as long as your theatre is wide) into the other.

Mime the title of a book, TV programme, or film for your friends to guess.

Earth matters

Much of what we see in the world around us is very beautiful. Isn't it sad when it is threatened by pollution? Here's a chance for you to do your bit for the world, and have fun at the same time.

Things to do
* Take photographs
* Neighbours: interview and make notes
* Contact council
* List possible solutions
* Write report
* Send to local newspaper

Environmental report

Pollution is all around us. There is smoke in the air, chemicals in the water, and litter on our streets. Identify an area near you which has been polluted and make a short video about it to show to your class. What caused the pollution? Interview your family and friends. Are they upset by the pollution? What do they want to do about it?

Stop press!

Write a report about the pollution and send it to your local newspaper. Say what the pollution is and how bad it is. If you have a camera, take some photographs. Talk to some local residents. You may even get your story printed!

Title and credits

To make a professional video, you need a title at the beginning and credits at the end. For an environmental report, why not use a stick to write the title in the ground and then film it? For the credits you could set the video up above your hand and film yourself writing the names of the people in the report and the name of the area you filmed.

Video hints and tips

★ To keep your picture steady, make sure you hold the camcorder with both hands. When you are filming a still shot, it is sometimes best to film in a kneeling position.
★ When you want to walk and film at the same time, try walking with your legs bent low to keep your body at an even level. This will ensure a smooth picture throughout.
★ Make sure you zoom in and out slowly to avoid any jerky movements.

★ When recording sound, test your microphone first. You will need to check how far away you need to stand from an interviewee.
★ Work out the questions you want to ask before you interview someone to avoid long silences.
★ Never film into direct light, as it will reflect off the lens and you will lose the picture.

  Plant a window box to brighten up your home.

It is best to plant seeds in the Spring. Throughout the year collect seeds and put them into clearly marked envelopes.

Try growing a seed indoors by planting it in a pot, giving it plenty of light and warmth, and watering it regularly.

Keep a record of the progress of your seeds. Draw pictures of them as they grow.

Planting a wilderness

Gather a variety of seeds from local plants and trees. Plant them in places, such as the edge of woods, by a roadside, or on waste ground. This will stop people leaving rubbish there and make the area more attractive. Visit the area regularly. Be patient – the seeds may take time to grow, but the results will be invaluable.

Acid rain test

Acid rain affects so much around us. To see how it affects plants, try this simple test. Take two healthy pot plants. Regularly spray and water one with water and one with a weak acid solution of one part vinegar, one part water.

Water

Acid

Check your plants daily. What happens to them?

And there's more . . .

Rock and roll

Geology is the study of the earth's structure. Look at rocks, stones, gems, and minerals in your area. Make drawings of the different types and write down your findings in a notebook. You may want to bring a few samples home.

Nature box

Make a display box by gluing together some matchbox drawers. Place cotton wool in each section to protect the display. Label the items and keep a note of when and where you found them.

Bring back the birds

Encourage winged wildlife into your garden by putting up a feeding table or nesting box for the birds. You could even put out a bird bath.

How many sources of **pollution** can you think of in ten minutes?

Friends

It's great to have **friends**! Whether you are indoors or out, you can always have fun **together**. Here are some **ideas** for you and your friends to enjoy.

Making friendship bracelets

Giving a friendship bracelet to a pal is a great way of showing them how much they mean to you. For a quick and easy bracelet, tape together five pieces of brightly coloured string at the top, and twist tightly. Next, hold both ends together and it will twist around itself. Knot the loose ends.

Wonder weave

You will need to spend a little more time on this bracelet, but it will be worth the hard work! Follow the steps carefully and make sure you give it to an extra-special friend.

You will need
- 5 pieces of coloured string
- Tape

1 Take five pieces of string of the same length and fold them in half. Tie a knot at the top to form a loop and tape it to a table.

2 Separate all the strands into their five colours. Weave the right-hand strand across the others and pull it tight.

Sleepover

Invite your friends to stay overnight. Here are some ideas to ensure they have a night to remember!

Top that!

Take a small pizza base, spread tomato sauce on it, and simply let your imagination go wild with weird and wonderful shaped vegetables, fruit, and cheese!

Corn-popping good!

With adult help, heat a small amount of cooking oil in a deep pan. When it is very hot, add half a cupful of corn, and shut the lid quickly. Shake the pan and listen to it pop! Add salt or sugar. **!**

Keep the lid on until all the corn has popped. You don't want it all over the kitchen!

Mark your friends' **birthdays** on a calendar to remind you.

Remember – over the first, under the second, over the third, and under the fourth.

3 Keep weaving the strand on the right to the other side until you reach the end. Be patient, it may take a long time!

4 When you have finished weaving, tie a knot in the end to secure it. Give the bracelet to a friend to remind them of you.

Biking adventure

A day out cycling with your friends can be great fun to plan. Get out the maps and outline a route, prepare plenty of food and drink, and remember to let an adult know where you are going and how long you will be!

And there's more . . .

Secret language

Do you ever want to tell a friend something in secret? Invent a secret language that only you and your friend can use and understand. You can use signs or code words, or try a code where you drop the first letter of every word and add it to the end of a word, followed by an "ay" sound. "Hello" would then become "ellohay"!

A tight squeeze!

Using chalk, draw a circle on the ground. Now see how many of your friends can stand inside the circle. Squeeze them all in!

Cheeky caricatures

Draw quick "head and shoulder" sketches of your friends. Exaggerate their features and have some laughs together.

Scary faces!

Tell a ghost story to some friends in a darkened room. Make a scary face and shine a torch suddenly underneath it. Watch them jump out of their skins!

Why not organize a trip to the **cinema** with your friends?

Sticks galore

What can you do with a bundle of sticks? The possibilities are endless! Sticks come in all **shapes** and **sizes** and collecting them is as much fun as using them for these great ideas!

You will need
- 6 x 2 m garden canes
- Large elastic bands
- 5 x 60 cm canes
- String
- 5 m x 1.5 m piece of calico or old sheet
- Fabric or poster paint

Tepee-building

With just a few canes and a sheet you can make an impressive tepee. Entertain your friends by inviting them to a tepee party!

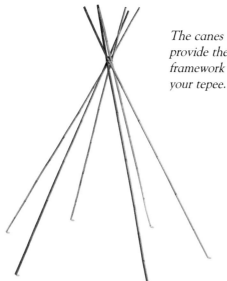

The canes will provide the framework of your tepee.

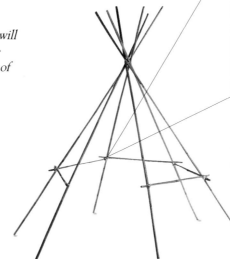

When attaching the smaller canes, wind the string around them lots of times and tie a tight knot.

1 Hold the six garden canes upright in a bunch and tie them together with elastic bands, about 40 cm from the top. Pull the canes out at the bottom until they are wide apart, as shown.

2 Use string to tie the five smaller canes, about halfway up in-between the larger canes. Leave one of the spaces without a small cane. This will eventually be the door of your tepee.

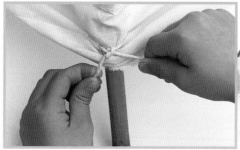

3 Wrap the fabric around the canes, making sure that the ends of the sheet meet on either side of the door so you can climb in. Tie the string tightly at the top. You may need a friend to help you.

4 Make two holes in the sheet by the base of each cane. Thread string through the holes and around the cane, then tie tightly. Do the same halfway up the canes, too.

Set up a **hurdle** race. Two upright forked sticks with a third lying across make a perfect hurdle!

If you are really quiet, you can watch animals and birds from the tepee without them seeing you.

5 Use a paintbrush to decorate the tepee with bright colours and bold patterns. Remember that the tepee is not waterproof, so put it away at night, or if it rains!

Put a waterproof sheet inside your tepee to sit on to keep you dry.

And there's more . . .

Stick insects

It may not look like a pet. In fact sometimes you may have difficulty seeing it at all! A stick insect can look like a stick or a curled-up leaf, and it makes a fascinating pet.

Stick ahoy!

Stand on a bridge with a friend and both drop a stick into the water on the upstream side. Run to the other side to see which stick appears first!

Stick raft

Make a raft by tying eight small sticks together with two underneath for support. Add a mast and a bright paper sail. Float it down a stream and watch it sail away in the wind!

Pick-a-stick

Take 20 wooden kebab skewers and paint five each yellow, red, blue, and green. Hold them in a bunch with the points resting on the floor, then release. Can you pick out a stick without the others moving? Score one point for a yellow, two for a blue, three for a green, four for a red. Take it in turns. Careful, a small twitch and you're out!

Limbo dance under a cane – how **low** can you go?

Money, money, money!

We can always think of ways to **spend** our money, but what about **making** some? Here are a few ideas for **earning** money and for making a safe place to keep it.

Papier mâché piggy bank

Keep your pocket money safe in this brilliant piggy bank. It's very simple to make, so you could even create an extra one as a present for a friend.

You will need

- Small, round balloon
- 2 cardboard tubes
- Yoghurt pot
- Scrap card and paper
- Sticky tape
- Wallpaper paste or PVA glue mixture (2 parts glue, 1 part water)
- Poster or acrylic paint
- PVA glue
- Black marker pen
- Pipe-cleaner

1 Blow up the balloon to make the pig's body. Cut the tubes in half and tape the four pieces together to form the legs. Mark a slot for the money.

2 Tape a yoghurt pot over the end of the balloon for the snout. Cut out two triangles of card for the ears. Tape the legs and ears to the balloon body.

3 Paste small pieces of scrap paper all over the pig, but be sure to leave the money slot area free. Cover the pig with several layers of paper and glue.

4 Leave the pig to dry overnight. When dry, stick a pin through the money slot to burst the balloon. Paint your pig with pink paint.

Paint the ears, snout and toes a darker pink.

When you want to spend your money, stick a blunt knife into the slot, turn the pig upside down, and coins will slide down the knife.

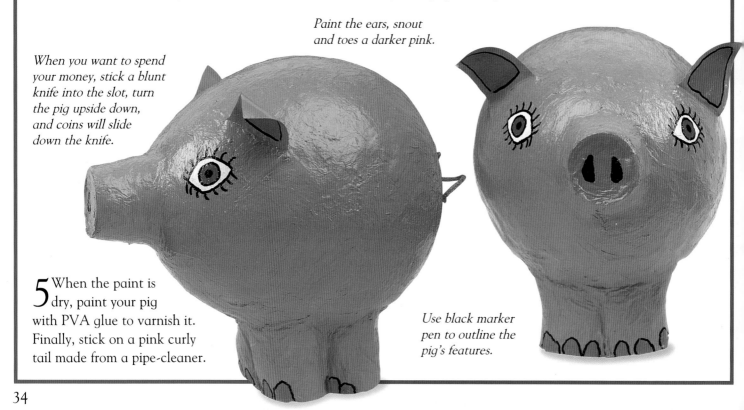

5 When the paint is dry, paint your pig with PVA glue to varnish it. Finally, stick on a pink curly tail made from a pipe-cleaner.

Use black marker pen to outline the pig's features.

Making money

Have you ever wished that you could make your own money? Then you could be really rich! Here's an easy way to create your own coins. They are made from salt dough, so don't try spending them!

You will need

- 300 g plain flour
- 300 g salt
- 1 tablespoon of vegetable oil
- 200 ml water
- Poster paint
- PVA glue

4 Leave the coins to cool, then paint them in bright, metallic colours. When the paint is dry, coat your coins with PVA glue.

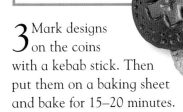

1 Set your oven to 180°C/350°F/Gas Mark 4. Mix the flour, salt, oil, and water in a bowl to form a soft dough.

2 Sprinkle some flour on the table and knead the dough until it is smooth and stretchy. Cut out circles for the coins.

3 Mark designs on the coins with a kebab stick. Then put them on a baking sheet and bake for 15–20 minutes.

Talents for sale

This is a great way to raise money for a good cause or charity. Make a list of all your family and friends. Ask each person to tell you one job that they can do well. It might be gardening, cleaning windows, baking a cake, or walking the dog. These are talents. The idea is to sell each person's talent, including your own, to someone else. The buyer gives the money for your charity and you complete the job.

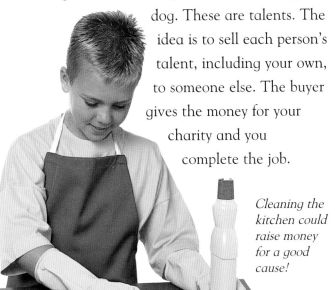

Cleaning the kitchen could raise money for a good cause!

And there's more . . .

Extra, extra!

Need some extra spending money? Why not offer to do a few chores around the house and garden – for a small fee of course!

Money-making money

Your piggy bank is good for storing coins, but if you are given a larger amount of money, a better place to keep it is in a bank or building society. The bank will pay you extra money, called interest, on the money that you save in your account.

Money for charity

Raise money for a local charity by organizing a sponsored event – a walk, a run, or even a sponsored silence! Think of something unusual, and encourage your family and friends to join in too.

Bigger and bigger

We may not realize it, but all around us things are growing – the leaves on the trees, the grass under our feet, and even our feet! Have a go at making things grow with these activities.

Growing beans

Normally we can't see what happens when a seed begins to grow, as it all takes place underground. However, if you grow a bean in a glass jar you can see exactly what happens and when.

1 Sandwich a bean or pea between the inside of a glass jar and a piece of blotting paper or cartridge paper. Don't use a cooked bean – it won't grow!

2 Pour water into the jar until the paper won't absorb any more. Keep the jar in a warm, dark place. Check it every day and add water regularly.

3 Soon you will see a root tip forming, followed by a little shoot. Move the jar into the light and the shoot will continue to grow.

Little feet – big feet

Ask everyone in your family to draw their feet. Cut them out and colour them in. Label whose they are so you don't forget. You could even display them on your wall! Six months later, do the same thing and compare sizes. Whose feet have grown the most?

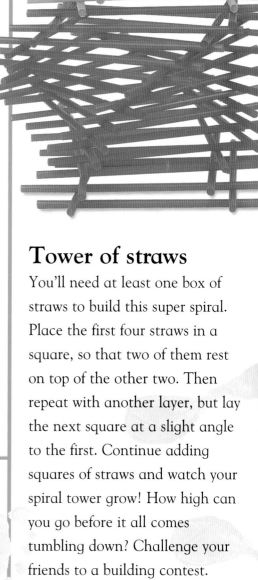

Tower of straws

You'll need at least one box of straws to build this super spiral. Place the first four straws in a square, so that two of them rest on top of the other two. Then repeat with another layer, but lay the next square at a slight angle to the first. Continue adding squares of straws and watch your spiral tower grow! How high can you go before it all comes tumbling down? Challenge your friends to a building contest.

Find out the **tallest** mountain in the world and the tallest building in the **world**.

Blow it up!

Copying a picture or enlarging it can be difficult, but if you follow the steps below you will get a much better result.

1 Select the picture you would like to copy. It could be a photograph or a drawing. Using a pencil, draw a grid of squares on a sheet of tracing paper and lay it over your picture.

2 To enlarge the picture, draw a faint copy of the grid onto your paper, but make the new grid squares several times larger. If you first want to copy the picture, copy the grid as it is.

3 In each square draw exactly what you can see in the corresponding square on the original. At the end, you should have an enlarged copy of the original picture. Colour it in to finish it off.

Sunflower challenge

Sunflowers are beautiful plants. They grow very tall and are an impressive sight, especially when several are grown together. Grow one in a pot as a present, or challenge your friends to see who can grow the tallest.

Hollyhocks are another flower that just grows and grows and grows.

1 Fill a pot with soil. Push a few sunflower seeds into the soil and water. Place a plastic bag over the pot top and secure it with an elastic band. Place in a warm, sunny place, then watch for that first shoot!

2 As your seedlings grow, you will have to transfer them to a bigger pot or plant them in the ground.

Exploration

It must have been wonderful to be an explorer, sailing round the world, **discovering** new lands, peoples, and animals. You can be an **explorer** too – and the best thing is that you don't have to **travel** far to do it!

Research a famous explorer

You can relive the discoveries of explorers like Christopher Columbus by reading about their voyages. Get out your books or go to the library and find out as much as you can about a famous explorer.

Mark your explorer's journeys on a photocopied map.

This map shows Columbus' routes to the Americas.

How did your explorer travel around? Draw a picture of the method of transport.

Draw your explorer and some things that would have been taken on the travels.

Map it out

Draw a map of the area where you live, marking roads and the main landmarks. Copy the layout of the streets from a local map, or walk round the area first and make a rough sketch before drawing your map.

Map symbols

Use picture symbols, like the ones shown here, to add information to your map, with a key to explain what they mean. The more you show, the more useful your map will be to someone else. Use a compass to work out where North is, then draw an arrow on the map pointing North.

Map of Baytown

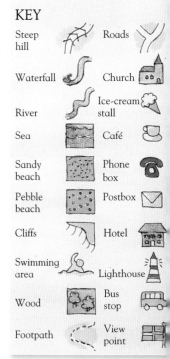

KEY

Steep hill		Roads	
Waterfall		Church	
River		Ice-cream stall	
Sea		Café	
Sandy beach		Phone box	
Pebble beach		Postbox	
Cliffs		Hotel	
Swimming area		Lighthouse	
Wood		Bus stop	
Footpath		View point	

Check that the symbols on your map match the ones on the key. Then you can colour in your map.

Which way is North?

Hold a compass in your hand. Keep it steady and make sure you are not standing near anything that is made of metal. Wait for the needle to stop moving. Slowly turn the compass until the coloured end of the needle is pointing to the "N". This is magnetic North.

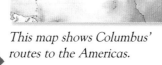

Add place and road names to your map. You could even mark your house with a special symbol.

Do you think someone else could find their way using your map?

And there's more . . .

Treasure hunt
Lay a treasure trail around your home. Set a clue that will lead your friends to another hidden clue, and so on. The last clue will lead them to the hidden treasure.

On the move
Can you design a vehicle to take an explorer around the world? It would need to travel on land and water, even underwater. It would have to climb mountains and ski over snow. It might even need to tunnel through rock. What would it use for fuel?

Capital cities
A good explorer should know their way around the world. How many countries and their capital cities can you learn?

Make your own compass
A magnetized needle will always swing around to point to magnetic North. Magnetize a needle and make your own compass.

You could add dots around your cork to show East, South, and West.

1 With the needle eye pointing downwards, stroke a magnet along a needle from top to bottom. Do this about 50 times.

2 Push the needle though a slice of cork. With a pen, draw an arrow on the cork, in the same direction as the needle point. This will be North.

3 Place the cork in a bowl of water, making sure that the bowl is on a flat surface. When the cork settles, the point of the needle will be pointing towards North. If you have a compass, you can use it to check that the needle is working.

If you were going **exploring**, which one **luxury** item would you take with you?

Festival fun

Festivals are always fun! There is lots of **food** and **dressing up**. Use these ideas to **celebrate** your own festival!

Gingerbread shapes

Gingerbread biscuits are made in Sweden for St Lucia's day on 13 December. Make some of these delicious biscuits and decorate them in lots of bright colours for your special occasion.

You will need

For the biscuits
- 175 g soft brown sugar
- 4 tablespoons golden syrup
- 115 g butter
- 340 g plain flour
- 2 teaspoons of ground ginger
- 1 teaspoon bicarbonate of soda
- 1 beaten egg

For the icing
- Water
- Icing sugar
- Food colouring

Gift stocking

Make this gift stocking and fill it with goodies to make a great birthday present for a friend or for a member of your family at Christmas. Decorate it with a design to suit the occasion or the theme of the festival. You could even cut out the person's name in felt and attach it with glue or thread.

1 Set the oven to 190°C/ 375°F/Gas Mark 5. Put the brown sugar, golden syrup, and butter in a saucepan and stir over a low heat until melted.

2 Stir the flour, ginger, and bicarbonate of soda together in a bowl. Mix in the syrup and beaten egg. Knead into a ball of dough and chill for 30 minutes.

3 Roll out the dough until it is about 0.5 cm thick. Cut into different shapes with pastry cutters, then bake in the oven for 10–15 minutes.

1 Cut out two stocking shapes from felt. Glue a rectangular flap of felt to the top of each stocking shape. Leaving the top open, pin and sew the two stocking pieces together, with the flaps on the inside.

2 Turn the stocking inside out and use pinking shears to give a decorative edge to the flaps. Decorate the stocking with a festive design made out of pieces of felt.

Select the colour of your felt to suit the occasion. Red, green, and white make jolly Christmas stockings.

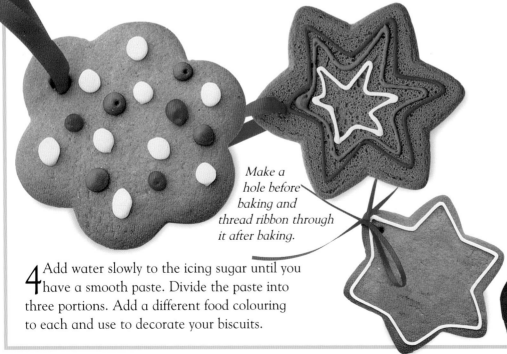

Make a hole before baking and thread ribbon through it after baking.

4 Add water slowly to the icing sugar until you have a smooth paste. Divide the paste into three portions. Add a different food colouring to each and use to decorate your biscuits.

Why not make a colourful costume to go with your mask?

Animal mask

Masks are popular at many festivals. Make an animal mask by covering a paper plate with lots of brightly coloured tissue paper. Add features, such as a nose or feathers. Remember to cut eye holes to see through!

Protection bracelet

During the *Raksha Bandhan* festival in Northern India, sisters give bracelets, called rakhis, to their brothers. They promise to look after their sisters in return. Make this bracelet out of coloured threads twined together (see pages 30-31).

Stick a disc of card in the centre and decorate it with colourful paper petals and beads.

Candle magic

Candles make a room feel mysterious. Make a candlestick, like this Jewish *Hanukkah* candle holder, out of modelling clay and decorate it with paint.

This ghost would be really scary on a dark Hallowe'en night!

Dressing up

Making costumes and dressing up in different disguises is all part of festival fun. This ghost is easy to make. Cut eye holes in an old sheet and draw on ghoulish features in black. Add black gloves, tights, and shoes and carry a chain! The lantern is simply a carved-out pumpkin.

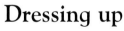

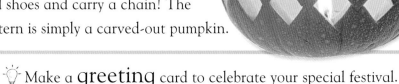

Make a **greeting** card to celebrate your special festival.

Move it!

Making things move, or appear to move, can **create** some great **effects**.

Make these moving projects and **impress** your family and friends!

The domino challenge

Stand your dominoes in a long, wiggly line, then gently knock over the last one. As the dominoes fall over one by one, it looks like a wave running along the line. For a really dramatic run, set up as many dominoes as you can find and design intricate patterns. Don't knock one over by mistake!

Flick book fun

How do you make still pictures move? Easy – draw lots of them and flick! This illusion takes patience, but it's great fun and very effective.

1 Cut out 16 cards. Draw a picture on the first, such as a stick man or a penguin on a pogo stick! On the next card, draw the same figure, but in a slightly different position.

Have you got the sh-sh-shakes?

It's best to have a really steady hand for this game. Challenge your friends to see who has the greatest control. Decorate a cardboard box with coloured paper, then follow the steps carefully to create your very own tremble tester!

You will need

- 1 x 40-cm length of 30-amp fuse wire
- 1 x 15-cm length of 30-amp fuse wire
- Small cardboard box with lid (a shoe box is ideal)

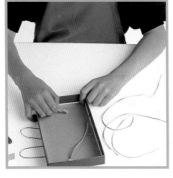

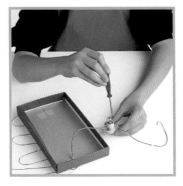

1 Make a series of bends in the 40-cm fuse wire. Form a loop at one end of the 15-cm wire and thread it onto the bendy wire. Push the bendy wire ends through the box lid.

2 Tape one wire end to the inside of the lid. Join one end of a 20-cm flex to the other end of the bendy wire and tape the join securely to the lid. Next, screw the bulb into the bulb holder.

3 Attach the two 20-cm flexes to the holder with a screwdriver, as shown. Make a hole in the centre of the lid for the bulb holder, push it through, and tape it in place.

4 Attach the free end of the 20-cm flex to a battery terminal. Join one end of the 55-cm flex to the other terminal. Make a small hole in the lid and push the flex end through from the inside.

Hold a broom beside you and **spin** around it while looking at the tip. Stop. Can you stand **still**?

2 Draw the figure on each card, but each time change its position slightly. Carefully plan the sequence of pictures so that it shows your character moving. Staple the cards together, then hold as shown and flick. Can you see your figure moving? The more pictures you have, the more effective the flick book will be.

And there's more . . .

Magnetic snakes

Draw a snake-shaped spiral onto some felt. Cut out and decorate. Tie a short piece of thread to a paper clip. Attach the clip to the snake's head and tape the end of the thread to a table. Tape a magnet to a ruler and gently wave it over the snake's head to see it dance!

Gliding hovercraft

Cut the top off a plastic bottle about 10 cm down and ask an adult to drill a 3 mm hole in its cap. Blow up a balloon, pinch the neck, and stretch the end over the cap. Let the balloon go, nudge the bottle top, and watch it glide away!

- Sticky tape
- 2 x 20-cm length of flex
- 3.5V bulb
- Bulb holder
- 1 x 55-cm length of flex
- 4.5V battery

You can make the game more difficult by putting tighter bends in the wire.

A buzzer can be used instead of a bulb.

For a special effect, decorate the top of the box with electric flashes.

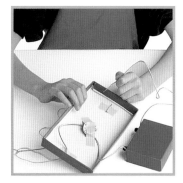

5 Put the battery inside the cardboard box and put the lid on. Join the free end of the 55-cm flex to the wire loop. Do this by twisting the flex wire tightly around the handle.

6 Challenge your friends to try and pass the loop from one end of the bendy wire to the other without touching it. There's no chance of cheating, as the bulb will light up if the wire is touched!

💡 The Sun seems to move across the sky – but does it really? Find out!

In the print shop

Turn your house into a **printer's** shop. Enjoy spending time making your own original **stencils** or become a **reporter** and print your very own newspaper!

You will need
- Box
- Card
- Paints

Fruity gift box

Brighten up a dull-looking gift box with this cheerful fruity stencil. It makes a great alternative to wrapping paper!

1 To make the stencil, carefully cut out an apple shape, including a stalk and leaf, from card.

2 Lay the stencil on the box and lightly dab the paint on with a thick brush, one colour at a time.

3 Repeat the stencil on all sides of the box. Put the lid on and repeat part of the stencil pattern where the lid overlaps it.

Stamp it out!

Print your own wrapping paper by stamping a design onto coloured paper. Why not plan the design so that it reflects a special occasion? Below are two different ways to make stamps.

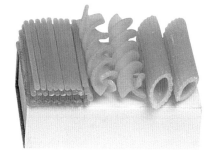

Sponge it!
Draw a simple design on to a household sponge. With adult help, cut around your design with scissors. **!**

Pasta patterns
Stick different shaped pieces of pasta on to the bottom of a matchbox with PVA glue.

Family news

Stop press! Keep your relatives up to date on all the latest family news with your own newspaper. Using either a computer or a pen, start with a large, bold headline about the biggest piece of news, like a wedding, a birthday, or the birth of a baby. Include a photo if you can. Write news of other family events or invite relatives to write in with their thoughts and print their letters. You could even include a puzzle, such as a crossword. Start with a single sheet of paper, photocopy it, and send it around the family. If it is popular, try making more pages by folding large sheets of paper in half, just like a real newspaper. Have fun being a reporter!

Include jokes, cartoons, and funny stories that will give everyone a laugh.

Dip the stamps into paint. Place carefully but firmly on to a piece of coloured paper, and remove.

For a sparkling finish, paint some PVA glue on to the paper and sprinkle the design with glitter.

And there's more . . .

Wrap it up!

Sponge paint on to the palms of your hands and the soles of your feet and stamp them on to a large sheet of paper – but don't walk through the house until you've washed them! This makes fantastic wrapping paper, or you could even turn it into a huge wall painting.

Baby feet

Stamp the side of your fist, with the little finger nearest the bottom, on to an ink pad and then on to a sheet of white paper. A tiny footprint! Add the toes by using your fingertips at the top of the print. Walk lots of baby feet across some paper and turn it into writing paper!

. . . it means it has gone to be **printed**.

In the jungle

Jungles are full of **exotic** animals and curious noises. Snakes slithering, **monkeys** screeching, and **shadows** all around. Visit this strange and exciting place without having to leave your house!

Jungle masks

Be a wild party animal – make these friendly, felt animal masks for a fancy dress party.

Practise moving about as your animal would do.

1 Decide what animal you'd like to be, then draw its face full-size on to a piece of paper. This is your mask template.

2 Using this template, cut out different coloured pieces of felt to make the various parts of the face.

3 Stick the felt pieces on to card. Cut out and assemble the pieces of your mask, then glue them all together. Tape a length of elastic to the back and pull it over your head to hold the mask in place.

Jungle snacks

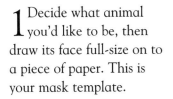

What sort of food might you find in the jungle? There would be plenty of grubs and bugs – but you might not fancy them! What about fruit and nuts? Combine different dried fruits and nuts to make some tasty snacks.

You can buy all sorts of dried fruits; try apricots, raisins, sultanas, and bananas.

You can add all sorts of nuts including Brazil nuts, almonds, pecans, and peanuts.

Avoid nuts if you have a nut allergy.

!

Animal shadows

Would you be afraid in the jungle at night? If you heard an animal howl, would you scream? If there was a rustling in the undergrowth, would you run? What if a strange shadow appeared on the wall of your tent? Shine a lamp on to the wall of your room, hold your hands in front of it, and have a go at making these animal shadows. Experiment by making up your own animals, real or imaginary.

Can you find out the size of the biggest **spider** in the world?

Imitate the sounds that your animal might make.

The beads help the snake to twist and slither about.

Attach handling strings as shown. For better control, loop the string around your thumb and little finger.

Slithery snake

Use acrylic paint to decorate a number of cotton reels with snake-like colours and patterns. If you don't have cotton reels, try toilet rolls instead. Add eyes and a forked paper tongue to one of them. String them onto some cord and put wooden beads between each section.

And there's more . . .

Tropical trees

Roll a large sheet of paper into a tube. Flatten it. Cut halfway down the flattened part and then cut halfway down both folds. Pull at the centre of the "leaves" and watch your tree grow!

Animal silhouettes

Trace the outlines of some wild animals from nature books. Colour them in black. Now ask your friends to guess what the animals are.

Research the rainforests

Find out all you can about rainforests. Contact a worldwide conservation organization to find out where they are, why they are so important, and why people are cutting them down.

Is it a bird? Is it a bat?

Hold your hands together as shown and move your fingers up and down to imitate a bird in flight or a bat flapping its wings.

Pretty peacock

Your forearm makes the bird's neck, your hand its head, and your fingers its eye and beak. Place an outstretched hand by your elbow to imitate wings.

By the book

Everyone should have **books** in their home. How else would you prop up a wobbly table? Or press flowers?! But seriously, whether you're into **reading** or **writing** books, they are a great pastime.

Creative bookbinding

Make this special notebook to record your thoughts and any funny jokes or stories you hear.

Make a book cover

1 Cover a notebook with fake leopard fur. Fold the material over the edges, trimming the corners at an angle so that they fold neatly. Glue in place.

2 Cut card to fit inside the front of the book, making sure it is just slightly smaller than the book itself. Glue the left-hand section over the fur.

You will need

For your notebook
- Notebook
- Covering fabric
- PVA glue
- Black card

For your bookplate
- White paper
- Dark-coloured felt-tip pen
- Rubber

For your bookmark
- Card
- Covering fabric
- Ribbon
- Double-sided sticky tape

Repeat step two at the back of the book, this time gluing the right-hand section.

☼ **Draw** a picture to illustrate an episode from one of your favourite **stories**.

Make a bookplate

Cut out a sheet of paper, giving the edges a decorative finish. You could cut wavy edges. Decorate using a stamp carved from a rubber and inked with a felt-tip pen.

If you like to draw, use your notebook for sketching, too.

Make a bookmark

Cover one side of a strip of card with material and fold over the edges. Use double-sided sticky tape to stick a second strip of material on the back.

THIS BOOK BELONGS TO

_____

SECRET!

DO NOT READ ANY FURTHER!

For added style, punch a hole in the end of the bookmark and thread a ribbon through before sealing the back.

And there's more . . .

Hear all about it!

Help someone who can't see very well by recording yourself reading a book or from a newspaper onto a tape. Give them a new tape each week.

Swap-shop

Organize an afternoon when all your friends meet and swap books.

True life story

Write a story or poem about something that has happened to you. If you have a computer, add illustrations and sound effects.

Boulder bookends

When you sit your books on the shelf do they fall over? Well, make bookends to prop them up. Find some heavy stones and stick them on top of each other to make an interesting shape. Why not paint it to look like a pirate!

Balance two books on your head. How far can you walk without them falling off?!

Worldwide

The world is such an exciting place, with so many different people, languages, foods, festivals, and customs. Explore our world and have an adventure – there is so much to discover!

Where in the world?

If you could visit 20 countries in an amazing once-in-a-lifetime holiday, where would you go? Plot your route on a world map or globe.

How long do you think it would take to complete your journey?

Worldwide picture

When family members and friends go on holiday abroad, they often send postcards back home. Collect all the postcards you can find and arrange them in a frame to make one big world picture.

Friends around the world

Would you like to have a friend who lives in another country? You could write to each other, send gifts on birthdays, and someday you may even meet up. To find a pen-pal, contact your local library for details. They may have the address of a pen-pal club that you can write to.

Mix and match flags

Every country in the world has its own flag. Make a selection of national flags and challenge your friends to pin them on a map beside the correct countries.

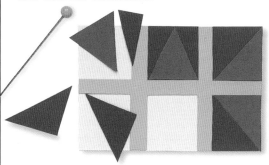

1 Cut out a small rectangular piece of plain card for each flag, then stick down coloured paper shapes to make the flag's design. Alternatively, you could draw the pattern on with coloured pens.

2 Tape a map pin or a long sewing pin to the edge of each of the flags. You could also design a flag for a country you have made-up and have a laugh when your friends try to place it!

Choose some flags that are well-known and others that are not.

How many ways can you find to say "hello" in other languages?

Mexican mealtime

It is always fun to try out new food. Make these quick and easy recipes for bean-filled taco shells and guacamole.

You will need

- 1 onion
- 1 carrot
- 1 garlic clove
- Cooking oil
- Half a teaspoon of chilli powder
- 400 g of chopped tomatoes
- 400 g of kidney beans
- Juice of a lemon
- Lettuce
- Taco shells
- Cheese

1 Finely chop an onion and carrot and crush a garlic clove. Heat a little cooking oil in a saucepan, then add the vegetables and cook until soft. Stir in half a teaspoon of mild chilli powder.

Don't use too much chilli powder – you don't want to blow your head off!

2 Next, add the tomatoes, the kidney beans, and the lemon juice. Simmer for 15 minutes, or until the sauce has thickened. Warm the taco shells in the oven for three minutes.

The lettuce will cool your mouth if the taco is too spicy!

3 To serve, put some shredded lettuce in the taco shell followed by a good helping of the bean mixture. Garnish with a little grated cheese. Make a side dish of guacamole and tomato relish to complete the meal.

The cheese will begin to melt all over the taco.

Side-dish delights

These tasty treats make great side dishes for your tacos, or you can make them on their own to eat as dips with tortilla chips.

Guacamole

Cut two avocados in half, scoop out the stone and peel off the skin. Cut the flesh into small pieces. Mash with a fork, then add the other ingredients. Mix it all together to make a great side dish.

You will need

- 2 avocados
- 1 skinned tomato
- Juice of a lime
- 1 clove of garlic (crushed)
- Salt and pepper

Guacamole dip makes a delicious snack if you're feeling peckish.

Tomato relish

Blend all these ingredients together to make a delicious salsa side dish.

You will need

- 1 finely chopped onion
- 5 skinned and finely chopped tomatoes
- 2 tablespoons of olive oil
- 1 tablespoon of wine vinegar

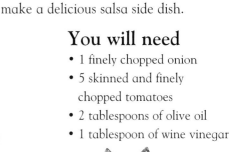

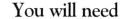

Design a poster advertising your favourite holiday destination.

Watery weekends

While away a **weekend** with these wonderful watery projects. From **watching** pond creatures to **making** seaside ice lollies, there is something here for everyone.

You will need

- Plastic funnel
- Wide plastic pipe
- Waterproof sticky tape
- String
- Torch
- Glass jar with lid
- Black plastic bag
- Elastic bands
- Bucket

Catch up on pond life

It's fascinating to watch the animals that live in a pond, but sometimes they can be very difficult to spot. Some small pond creatures are attracted to light. This clever pond-life viewer uses the light from a torch to lure the animals into an underwater trap. Then you can get a good look at them!

1 Push the narrow end of the funnel into the pipe and tape it in place. Loop string around the pipe and tie to make a handle.

2 Put a lit torch into the jar and screw the lid on. Place the jar in the pipe, so that the light shines through the funnel.

Everlasting aquarium

These fish will never need feeding and the water won't need to be changed either – because there isn't any! Glue the pebbles to the lid of the jar. Make the fish from card and hang them from the inside of the lid with thread. Stick scenery made from card to the bottom of the jar. Paint seaweed and bubbles on the outside surface of the jar.

You will need

- Glass jar
- Pebbles
- Glue
- Card
- Thread
- Acrylic paint

Underwater volcano

In this experiment the coloured, hot water rising through the clear, cold water in this jar looks like an erupting volcano.

You will need

- String
- Small glass bottle
- Hot and cold water
- Red food colouring
- Large glass jar

1 Cut a piece of string, about 30 cm long. Tie both ends of the string around the neck of the small bottle to make a handle.

2 Ask an adult to fill the bottle with hot water. Then add a few drops of food colouring to dye the water bright red.

? Did you know that **two-thirds** of the earth's surface is covered with **water**?

3 Fasten the plastic bag over the open end of the pipe with elastic bands. Lower the trap into a pond and leave it overnight. In the morning, lift the trap out and pour the contents of the plastic bag into a bucket to see what you have caught!

Water melon ice lollies

An ice lolly is an ice lolly – or so you would think. But just wait until your friends see these stunning seaside lollies. Made with melon shapes and fruit juice, they take some licking!

Cut seaside shapes from the melon using biscuit cutters or a knife and lay them in the lolly moulds. Fill the moulds with fruit juice, then pop them in the freezer for two hours.

To remove the lolly, hold the frozen lolly moulds upside-down under a running tap.

You will need

- Melon
- Lolly moulds
- Orange or lime juice

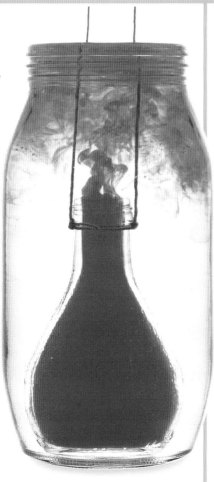

Use the string handle to lower the bottle carefully into the jar of cold water.

3 Pour cold water into the large jar until it is three-quarters full. Lower the bottle of hot water into the jar and watch what happens. It really does look like an erupting volcano, doesn't it?

And there's more . . .

Bending water

Pull a comb through your hair several times. Turn on a tap and hold the comb close to the stream of water. See how the water bends!

Water fountain

Fill one-third of a glass bottle with water. Make a hole in the cap and push a straw through. Surround the hole in the lid, around the straw, with modelling clay to keep it airtight. Adjust the straw so that it is near the bottom of the bottle. Flatten the end of the straw and blow. Take your mouth away and watch the fountain!

In the swim

Sign up for life-saving lessons at your local swimming pool. It's a great way to meet people and you'll learn a valuable skill, too.

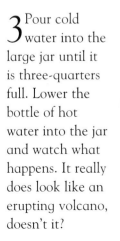

 Have a **race** where the runners hold a cup of water over their heads. How much water will be left?

Let's party!

You don't need a reason for a **party!** Just **invite** your friends round and have a really **great time** with these brilliant party ideas.

Be as imaginative as you like with your design. Try building the decorations up in layers to give a 3-D effect.

Fruity cocktail

Purée six strawberries in a blender, asking an adult to help you, then add 150 ml of cranberry juice and 150 ml of orange juice. Pour the mixture into glasses, then add some ice cubes and slices of orange and apple. Finish off each fruit cocktail with a brightly coloured straw.

Party invites

Make these extra-special party invites to send to your friends.

You will need

- Silver card and coloured card
- Cotton wool
- Glue
- Double-sided sticky tape
- Coloured thread or wool
- Streamers

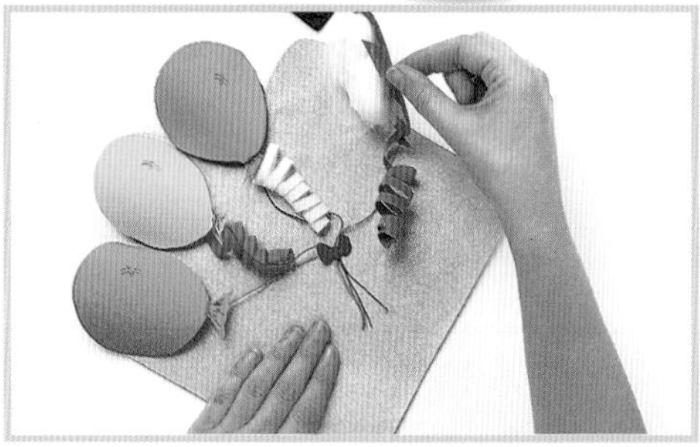

1 Fold a piece of silver card in half. Cut four balloon shapes from coloured card. Glue cotton wool behind each one, then stick it to the card with tape.

Get everyone to **tell** a joke or a **funny** story to get the party going.

Design a cake

Melt the chocolate in a bowl placed over warm water and then blend in the sour cream. Using a spatula, cover the cake. Leave it to set, then decorate!

We used sliced almonds, cherries, and sweets to make these decorations.

You will need

- Sponge cake
- 115 g milk chocolate
- 2 tablespoons of sour cream
- Sweets, nuts, and fruit for decoration

Rainbow paper chains

These paper chains make great party decorations. Cut some strips of coloured paper 20 cm long and 2 cm wide. Glue the ends of one strip together to make a loop. Thread the next strip through the loop, then glue its ends together, and so on.

Create a rainbow party atmosphere using balloons, decorations, and coloured lights.

Make sure you have some prizes ready as the treasure.

Cut a tab on either side of the balloons to make them easier to stick down.

And there's more . . .

Treasure hunt

Draw a room floor plan. Get your friends to mark an "X" where they think treasure is hidden. Reveal whose "X" is closest to the treasure, then give that person two minutes to find it!

All change

Everyone sits in a circle around you. Give an instruction, such as, "Everyone with blue eyes change places". While they do this, nip into an empty seat. The person left without a seat then sits in the centre. "All change", means everyone must change places.

2 Cut and remove the silver card around the top of the balloons. Stick on lengths of thread to make the balloon strings and add some streamers.

Make a small **gift** for each of your friends to **thank** them for coming to your party.

Bright ideas

There are many great inventions – the **telephone**, the light bulb, and the television. Here are some **bright** ideas that you can investigate or make.

Your great-grandparents may have used a wind-up gramophone like this.

Past inventions

Have a good hunt round your home. Which inventions are new, and which have been around for a long time? Discover more about the objects you find by asking your parents and grandparents if they had one when they were younger.

Mini disc player

What can you find around the house that has been invented since you were born?

Ask your parents and grandparents how they used to play music.

Cascade of chocolate

If you feed chocolate balls or marbles in at the top, they will cascade down through the tubes and pop out at the bottom.

You will need
- Cardboard tubes
- Cereal box with front cut off
- Yoghurt pot, cut in half
- Glue
- Wooden kebab skewers
- Dowelling
- Elastic band
- Matchsticks
- Poster paint
- Cling wrap
- Chocolate balls

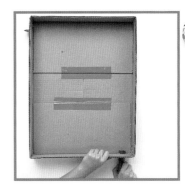

Elastic fits into groove in pinger.

1 Insert a tube into the top of the box. At the bottom of one side, make a hole for the balls to come out. Stick the yoghurt pot over the hole.

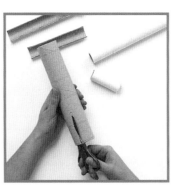

2 Cut the tubes to different lengths. Cut some in half lengthways to make slides. Make a hole in some tubes for the ball to drop through.

3 Plan the tube routes before gluing them down. Make tubes that swivel by taping skewers to them. Stick these through the box.

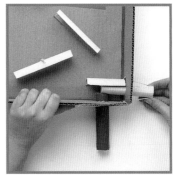

4 Make a "pinger" out of dowelling and cut a groove in one end. Cut a hole in the side of the box near the top tube. Glue a slide underneath.

5 Thread the elastic band ends through holes either side of the main hole and secure with two pieces of matchstick. Insert the pinger.

? Did you know that the first **motor car** was built as early as **1885** by Karl Benz?

6 Now paint your chocolate machine in bright colours. Finally, cover the front of the box with cling wrap. To work the machine, drop a ball down the top tube, pull back the pinger, then let go and watch what happens!

Make sure that the box sides are not too high. The tube edges need to fit flush against the cling wrap.

For extra strength, stick a cardboard strip across the front of the box to hold each swivelling tube and push the skewer through it.

Space-age super bike

Imagine a world, far out in space, where there are no roads. All the methods of transport – cars, buses, and lorries – travel above the surface of the ground. Can you design a space-age bike to use on this planet? What shape would it be? How would it be powered? What would it be made of?

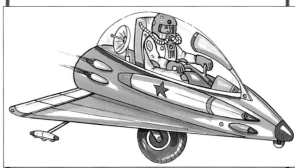

And there's more . . .

Weather maker

Invent an imaginary weather machine to make clouds and rain when you are in school, and sunshine when you are on holiday. What ingredients would you need to feed into the machine?

The power of paper

Using just one newspaper and a roll of sticky tape, can you build a structure with a platform and legs which will support the weight of a bag of sugar?

Research an inventor

Michael Faraday, "the father of electricity", invented the dynamo, the first electricity generator, in 1831. Find out about Faraday and his inventions.

? Did you know that skateboards were invented by surfers in the 1960s so they could surf on land.

Colour madness

Everywhere you look there are different colours, and there are many exciting ways to create or **change** them. Find out why there's more to **colour** than meets the eye!

How to turn a pretty white rose . . .

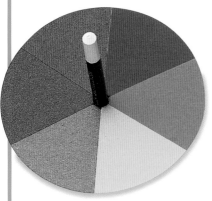

Colour mixer

Experiment with colour-mixing. This super spinner uses the primary colours, red, yellow, and blue, and the secondary colours, orange, green, and purple.

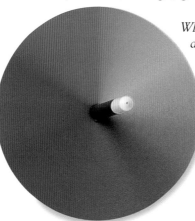

When a primary colour is mixed with another primary colour it forms a secondary colour of either orange, green, or purple.

1 Draw a circle onto card and divide it into six equal segments, using a protractor. Colour the segments in this order: red, orange, yellow, green, blue, and purple.

2 Push a pencil through the centre of the circle. Stand the pencil upright and spin it as fast as you can. What happens to the colours as the wheel speeds up?

Tie-dye today!

How would you like to design your own clothes? Tie-dyeing is a quick and easy way to jazz up those old white T-shirts, and you can choose any colour or pattern you want!

You will need
- White T-shirt
- Cold water dye
- String
- One or two marbles

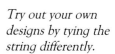

For a stripy effect, roll the T-shirt up from sleeve to sleeve, then tie the string at regular intervals.

1 To make the circular design, tie the marbles in the middle of a T-shirt. Next, use string to tie up sections of T-shirt at intervals.

2 Mix the cold water dye in a bowl and soak the shirt for one hour. Make sure you wear rubber gloves, as it can be a messy business!

3 Wring out the T-shirt and rinse well under cold water. Cut the string from the shirt and hang it up to dry.

Try out your own designs by tying the string differently.

 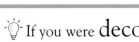 If you were **decorating** your room, which colours would you use? **Draw** a plan of your new room.

White to pink

Place a freshly cut white rose in a glass containing water and red food colouring. Leave in a warm room and examine after two or three hours.

. . . into a beautiful pink one !

And there's more . . .

Hidden colours

Cut out strips of blotting paper or cartridge paper. Using water-based felt-tip pens or water-soluble ink, draw a circle of colour in the middle of each strip. Hold the ends of the strips in a dish of water. What happens as the water slowly rises up the paper?

Choosy insects

Try this experiment to see if insects are attracted to some colours and not others. Cut different-coloured flower shapes from card, including a black and a white one. Put a drop of syrup in the centre of each, then place outside and observe what happens.

Rainbow magic

Sometimes after rain, a rainbow appears in the sky. However, you don't have to wait for it to rain to make your own rainbow!

You will need
- Shallow dish
- Mirror
- Modelling clay
- Water
- Torch
- White paper

1 Position the mirror in the dish at an angle and fix it in place with modelling clay. Half fill the dish with water.

2 Shine a torch on to the section of mirror under the water. Hold the paper above the dish, as shown, to catch the reflection of the torch light. Change the angle of the torch to improve the image.

The white light from the torch splits into rainbow colours.

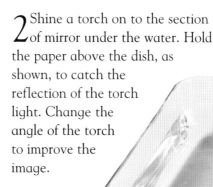

 Do a car **survey** in your area to find out the most **popular** colour of car.

59

Super spy

The **secret** of being a good spy is that you should be the last person anyone **suspects**. So, try to **act** completely normally and keep all your hi-tech equipment well **hidden!**

Secret Code

A B C D E F G H I J K L
j k l m n o p q r s t u

M N O P Q R S T U V W
v w x y z a b c d e f

X Y Z
g h i

Cracking codes

Secret codes are a must in spy work. Here is a simple one to start with. Write out the alphabet, then write out another below it, but start it ten letters ahead, as shown. Now write your message replacing the letters of each word with their code letters.

The receiver must have the code in order to read the message. Use the first two letters, A and J, as initials in a false name at the end of the letter.

Periscope power

If you need to spy over walls or look round corners, this periscope will come in handy. All you need are a couple of large drink cartons and two small mirrors.

1 Cut and remove the carton top. Draw two right-angled triangles on one side of the carton, as shown, with a double line along the diagonal edges. Ask an adult to cut along these lines to make two slots.

2 Repeat step 1 on the other side of the carton. Make sure the slots are directly opposite each other on both sides. Insert and tape a small mirror into each pair of slots with the mirrors facing each other.

Invisible writing

Write your message on a white piece of paper with a white crayon. Your friend will be able to read it simply by painting it with a weak paint solution.

You can also write with lemon juice, which appears when heated on a radiator or with a warm iron.

Go in disguise

A disguise helps you to mix with people without them recognizing you. Good use of clothes and make-up will change the way you look.

Dark glasses or a hat will help to hide your face.

Start a **detective** agency. Make a company identity card and **keep** a notebook of suspicious events.

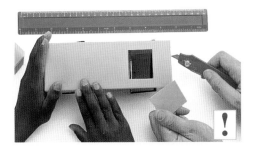

3 Decide which will be your top mirror and draw a square on the front of the carton, right in front of the mirror. Ask an adult to cut the square out.

Cut the base off another carton and tape it over the open end.

4 At the back of the carton, cut out a small viewing hole. The hole must be opposite the bottom mirror.

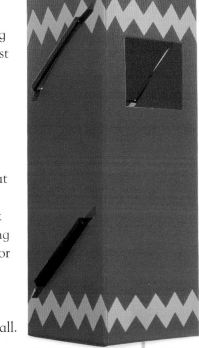

5 Place your periscope so that the square hole is above a wall. Look through the viewing hole. The top mirror will reflect on to the bottom mirror whatever is on the other side of the wall.

And there's more . . .

Use your head

When you are going out, shut the door, then pull a single hair from your head – ouch! Carefully wet the ends of the hair, then stick one end of the hair to the door and the other end to the door frame. When you return, check whether the hair has been disturbed.

Door alarm

When you are sitting in your room attending to spy business, close the door and place a small object on the handle. If anyone tries to open your door, the object will fall off and warn you.

Finger the culprit

Has someone borrowed your car without asking? Check for fingerprints to find the culprit. With a paintbrush, lightly dust talcum powder on to the surface of the car. Now, gently blow the talc away. If there is a fingerprint there, the talc will stick to it. Use a magnifying glass to examine any fingerprints.

See how to take a suspect's fingerprints on page 93, then check the fingerprints against the evidence.

Use hair gel to alter your hair style.

Highlight the wrinkles with white paint.

1 Use make-up to add wrinkles and shade areas of your face to change the way you look.

2 Frown, and then use brown face paint to draw wrinkles where your face creases. Add brown under your eyes too.

3 Make your eyebrows thicker and darker. Add stubble and a moustache. No-one will know you!

String things to do

Without **string** our world would fall apart! Here are some wonderful **ideas** to try using string – but be careful not to **tie** yourself in **knots**!

You will need
- Embroidery hoop
- 3.5 m of ribbon
- 6 m of string or cord
- Sticky tape
- Glue
- Assorted beads
- Coloured feathers

Colourful dreamcatcher

This great idea comes from a Native American custom of hanging dream catchers over sleeping areas. Make one to decorate your bedroom.

1 Wrap the hoop in ribbon, then tape. Make a loop at one end of the string. Pass the string around the hoop, then back through the loop.

2 Holding the loop in the centre of the hoop, continue wrapping the string around the hoop to form "spokes". Tie the end to the hoop.

3 Weave string through the spokes, tying a knot each time you cross a spoke. You can add beads at this stage. Glue the knots and leave to dry.

Decorate your dream catcher with coloured feathers and hang it up with a ribbon.

Make a string **printer**. Glue string around a bottle. Add **paint**, then roll across your paper!

Acrobatic water

Challenge your friends to make water walk the tightrope. Tie one end of a length of string to a spoon and the other to a jug, as shown.

Lift the jug up high and pull the string tight. Pour gently and watch as the water runs along the string!

Skipping superstar

Can you skip with the rope going backwards? What about crossing your arms while the rope is moving?

Figure of eight

Learn to tie some nifty knots. This knot is great for loops as it is quick to tie and strong. First cross the left end over the right and under, then cross the right end over the left and under.

Borrow a library book and get knotting!

All ears

Make your own mobile phone by connecting two tins or plastic cups with string. Pierce a hole in the base of each cup. Thread string through each hole and secure with a knot on the inside.

Long-distance call

Make sure your telephone string is pulled tight, while you speak into one end and a friend listens at the other.

Long narrow tins work the best.

String mats

Cut out a circle of stiff card. Cover one side with PVA glue or double-sided sticky tape. Taking some coloured string, start in the centre of the circle and work outwards to create a spiral of string.

Play **tug-of-war** with two teams pulling on either end of a length of rope. Who will fall over first?   63

Chamber of horrors

Freak out your friends the next time they come round to your house, with this collection of ghostly **ghouls**, and scary **spiders!**

Tasty spiders

Make these spiders and invite your friends over for a creepy crawly feast. First set the oven to 200°C/400°F/Gas Mark 6.

You will need

- 250 ml water
- 3/4 teaspoon of salt
- 100 g butter
- 150 g plain flour
- 4 eggs
- 1 beaten egg
- Whipped fresh cream
- Chocolate chips

Batty bat game

One person, the bat, sits blindfolded in the middle of a circle. The aim of the game is to quietly walk towards the centre and try to steal a prize that the bat is guarding. If the bat hears someone and points at them, they are out. The person who gets the prize is the winner.

1 Gently heat the water, salt, and butter in a pan. When the butter has melted and the mixture bubbles, remove the pan from the heat and add the flour.

2 Beat until the mixture leaves the side of the pan. Allow to cool slightly. Beat the eggs and add bit by bit, while continuing to stir the mixture.

3 Fit a nozzle on to a piping bag. Place the bag in a jug, as shown, and fill it with mixture. Twist the top of the bag making sure that no air is trapped inside it.

Cut the round shapes in half, fill with cream, add the legs, then more cream. Chocolate chips make excellent eyes!

Why not pipe a chocolate-icing spider's web on to a plate?

4 Pipe shapes on to the baking tray. Make thin, bent shapes for the legs and round shapes for the bodies. Brush with the egg and bake for 20–25 minutes.

5 Once cooked, gently prick each shape. Leave to cool and then decorate.

Blood suckers!

Become a vampire by whitening your face, adding red and black make-up around your eyes, and painting your lips bright red. Pretend fangs will complete your blood-sucking vampire look!

Haunted house

Make a super-scary haunted house from just a cardboard box and three simple bulb circuits. Use dark paint for the inside of the house, to give an extra-creepy, night-time effect, and fill it with spooky spirits and ghostly ghouls. When the house is completed, flick the switches and watch the eerie lights glow.

You will need
- Large cardboard box
- 1 m wire cut into 9 equal pieces
- Three 1.5V bulbs in holders
- Glue
- Three 1.5V batteries
- Plastic tape
- White and coloured card
- Coloured pens
- Pipe-cleaners
- Paint
- Coloured cellophane
- Three switches, each made from a piece of card, with a split pin on each end, and a steel paper-clip joining them.

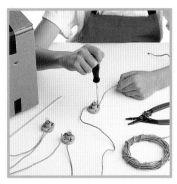  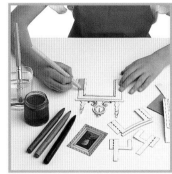 

1 Tape the top flaps to the sides of the cardboard box. Connect two wires to each bulb holder. Make holes in the top left side of the box and the two bottom corners at the back.

2 Glue a bulb holder next to each hole, inside the box. Thread the wires through the holes. Connect a switch and a battery to each pair of wires with tape. Join the switch to the battery with wire and tape.

3 Draw some furniture, a fireplace, a staircase, and a door on thin card. Cut them out and colour. Make lots of spiders out of pipe-cleaners and ghosts from coloured card.

4 Paint the inside of the box. To make the fire, cut an arch from card. Tape cellophane flame shapes across the arch, then paint the card the same colour as the inside of the box.

5 Stick the fireplace to the cardboard arch and tape in one corner, in front of a bulb. Put the open door in front of the bulb in the other corner so the light shines through. Stick the furniture in position and add the spiders and ghosts, making sure a ghost is in front of the remaining bulb. Turn on the bulbs and the spooky scene will glow eerily.

Paper power

There are endless ways to **cut** and fold paper to **create** decorations, **make** models, and **play** games. So start **folding** and have **fun**!

It's raining frogs!

Here's an idea that will get you folding, and when you have finished you can play the game! Make a large blue pond out of paper or card and decorate with cut-outs of lily pads and flowers. Then fold your frogs and make them jump!

The larger the piece of paper, the easier it is to fold.

1 Take a square of paper and fold the left and right sides into the centre. Fold the two top corners into the centre, crease, then unfold.

2 With the creases as a guide, turn the corners in on themselves, as shown. Fold the left and right edges of the paper into the centre.

4 Fold the bottom corners of the model into the centre, crease and unfold. Next, turn the corners in on themselves as in step 2.

5 To make the back legs of the frog, lift the two points at the base of the model and pull them up and to the side so that they now lie flat.

Thunderclap banger

Did you know you could make a loud bang with a piece of paper? Make this fantastic paper banger and surprise your friends with the effect!

1 Take a piece of paper measuring 30 x 40 cm and fold the longest edges together. Crease, then open out again. Now fold the four corners to the centre, as shown and crease.

Experiment with different paper thicknesses for the best bang.

2 Fold the model along the centre fold. Next, fold in half, taking the left corner point over to the right. Crease then open up.

3 Fold both top corners down using the middle crease as a guide. Fold the model in half backwards, along the middle crease.

  How many times can you **fold** a piece of **paper** in half? Have a go – can you fold it more than eight?

3 Pull down the pointed flaps at the top, so that they stick out at both sides. Crease. You now have the frog's head and legs.

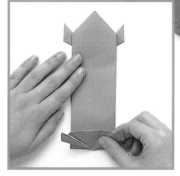

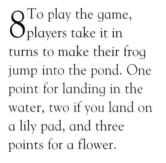

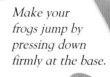

Make your frogs jump by pressing down firmly at the base.

6 Fold the top flaps in half as shown. Next, take the corners of the bottom flap and fold downwards, as shown. Crease all folds.

7 Now, fold the body four times to make a concertina shape – start with a backward fold at the bottom and work up.

8 To play the game, players take it in turns to make their frog jump into the pond. One point for landing in the water, two if you land on a lily pad, and three points for a flower.

The secret is in the flick of the wrist. Practice makes perfect!

4 Hold the banger firmly by the two top corners, as shown, and flick it down sharply. Be careful not to frighten yourself the first time you do it!

Stained glass windows

Real stained glass is expensive, but this stained-glass pattern is just as striking and very simple to make. Stick these amazing cut-outs on a window and see them shine!

1 Fold a square of black or dark paper in half to make a triangle. Then fold it in half twice more to make a smaller triangle. Now cut shapes out of each of the three edges.

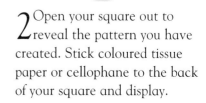

2 Open your square out to reveal the pattern you have created. Stick coloured tissue paper or cellophane to the back of your square and display.

67

Up in the air

What is it that we can't see, touch, or taste, but is all around us? Air, of course. We hardly notice it, yet we would die without it.

Bird-watching

Have you ever watched birds gliding effortlessly through the air? They are always on the move, looking for food or places to nest, and are fascinating to watch. Did you know they use rising, hot air to lift them high in the sky? Borrow a bird guide from the library to help you identify any birds that you see.

Keep a record book of the birds in your area. Write down the date, the type of bird, and where you saw it.

Flying high

Enjoy hours of fun making and flying this fantastic kite.

You will need

- 48-cm square of thin carrier-bag plastic
- Sticky tape
- Acrylic paints
- Thin strips of plastic
- 2 x 46-cm garden canes
- 90 cm of cord
- Large ball of string
- Small stick for handle

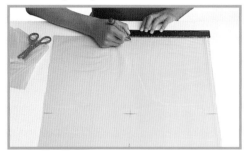

1 Fold the plastic in half to find the centre. Make three marks in a line, 14 cm from the top, and three down the centre, as shown. Join the outer marks to make a diamond shape. Cut the kite out.

2 Tape the corners. Stick two tape patches on the centre line, 11 cm and 41 cm from the top. Ask an adult to cut a slit in both. Fold over the corners, and punch a hole in each one.

Balloon-propelled rocket

Make this colourful tissue-paper rocket and watch it fly across the room!

1 First blow up a long balloon and wrap a sleeve of tissue paper loosely around it. Decorate the tissue paper so that it looks like a rocket.

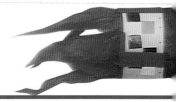

? Did you know that "kite" is also the name of a **bird of prey?**

Tie the string to the stick handle and wind it up, ready for flying the kite.

Flying in circles

Insects come in all colours, shapes, and sizes. Use modelling clay to make some of your favourite flying insects and create a colourful mobile.

Cut out a strip of card and decorate it with clouds and a sun. Tape the card ends together to form a circle. Use thread to attach the insects to the circle, add ribbon to hang it up, and hey presto – your very own insect mobile!

Insect alert

How many different kinds of insects can you spot flying around where you live? See if you can find out what they are called.

Make sure the canes are placed on the unpainted side.

3 Paint the kite. Cut out plastic strips for the tail and punch holes in one end. Thread on to a cane. Push both canes through the holes in each corner of the kite, as shown. Tape the cane ends.

4 Thread the cord ends through the two slits from the painted side, and knot to the cane. Turn the kite cane-side down. Tie a loop in the cord, as shown. Attach the string to the loop and knot.

And there's more . . .

Kick football

How long can you keep a football in the air without using your hands or arms?

Head in the clouds

Lie on the ground and look up at the sky. Is it a bird? Is it a rabbit? Use your imagination to see all sorts of shapes in the clouds.

Toy parachute

Tape thread to each corner of a square of thin carrier-bag plastic. Knot the free ends of the threads together and attach a small ball of modelling clay. Drop and watch it float gently down!

2 Tape a straw lengthways along the top of the rocket sleeve. Thread string through the straw. Tie the string to two chairs to make the rocket runway.

3 Now remove the first balloon and blow up another. Without tying the end, insert this balloon into the rocket sleeve and . . . **let go!**

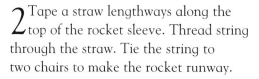

? Did you know that there are approximately **8,700** bird **species** in the world?

Animal magic

From bumble-bees to **tigers**, the **animal** kingdom is an amazing place to **explore**. Enjoy it!

Cattle stockade

This is a game for five or more players. One person is the bull. The other players link hands and form a circle, called a stockade, around the bull, who tries to escape by crawling over or under the players' arms. The stockade must stop the bull from escaping without breaking the ring. Once the bull escapes, he joins the stockade and chooses someone else to be the bull.

If you have lots of people, you can have several bulls in the stockade.

Bouncing bumble bees

You may not like real insects buzzing around your room, but you'll love these bees – they're so irresistably fluffy!

You will need
- Card
- Yellow and black wool
- Pipe-cleaners
- Glue
- Elastic

1 Cut out two rings of card and wind wool around them, going through the hole each time. When finished, cut through the wool, as shown.

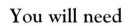

2 Tie a length of elastic tightly around the wool at the centre of the rings. Cut the rings away and fluff the wool into a ball.

3 Add pipe-cleaner legs and wings made from card. Make two eyes from circles of black and white card and stick in place.

Hang the bee up by the elastic and let it bounce!

🔆 Test your friends! **Choose** a **letter**. How many animals can you think of that begin with that letter?

Who goes there?

Make plaster casts to record animal tracks that you find in the mud or sand. Practise by making casts of your hands in self-hardening clay first.

You will need
- Self-hardening modelling clay
- Strip of card and paper-clips
- 420 g plaster of Paris
- 300 ml of water

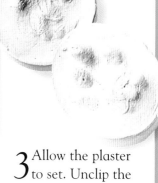

1 Find a print or make one of your own in clay. Place a strip of card in a circle around the print and secure with a paper-clip.

2 In a bowl, mix plaster of Paris with water to form a smooth, runny mixture. Pour it into the circle to a depth of around 2.5 cm.

3 Allow the plaster to set. Unclip the card and carefully lift the plaster. Leave for 24 hours to harden.

Tiger, tiger

Do you have a favourite wild animal? Find out all you can about it. Where does it live? How long does it live for? What does it eat? Collect pictures too. Make a large poster with all your information. Include poems and stories about your animal.

Footprints in the sand

When you next walk along the beach, watch out for prints in the sand. Can you identify them? Look back at your own footprints – can you walk in a perfectly straight line?

Can you notice any difference between the footprints of an animal with long legs and those of an animal with short legs?

And there's more . . .

Stick around!

Make animal shapes out of modelling clay. Allow to harden, then paint. Glue magnets to the back and they're ready to stick on your fridge!

All mixed-up

Draw a picture of an imaginary animal. Give it the head of one animal, the body of another, and the legs of a third. Paint it in crazy colours and give it its own unique name. Try combining the names of all the animals you've used.

Which animal would you be more afraid of, a **carnivore** or a **herbivore**? Why?

Making history

Who were your great-grandparents? Where did they live? What jobs did they have? Finding out about your **family** history can be really fascinating!

Tales to tell

Older members of your family, such as your grandparents or elderly neighbours will have some great stories to tell about their life when they were young. Ask them if you can record some of their childhood memories. How different was their life compared to your own?

Remember to take along a blank tape!

History in the making

What happens today will be history tomorrow. Take photographs and write an account of the important occasions in your life. It will be a fantastic record for future generations, and great to look back on when you are older.

A digital camera is a great way to record photos for storing on your computer.

Photos galore!

Collect photographs of yourself, your family, and your friends to make a really spectacular photomontage. Use a variety of photos, such as pictures taken at school, on holiday, or at home. Choose a piece of card that will fit into your chosen frame. Arrange your photos on the card and then stick them down.

Discard distracting background by cutting out just the part of the photograph you want.

You can achieve interesting shapes by cutting around figures or objects.

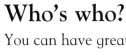

Who's who?

You can have great fun and a lot of laughs looking through your family's old photograph albums! Can you recognize members of your family? How are their clothes and the things around them different from today?

What is the oldest photograph you can find?

Do you look like any of your relatives?

What is the most recent photograph you can find?

💡 How far back can you trace your **family?** Can you go back to your great, great, great-grandparents?

And there's more . . .

What's in a name?

How did your town get its name? Does it have a meaning? If you had to rename it what would you suggest and why?

Happy Birthday!

Research the important facts that have taken place on your birthday in the years gone by. Who else was born on that date?

Collectables

Collections of objects can show us how life has changed over the years. Start your own collection and update it regularly.

Tree of life

Make your own family tree. Find photographs of yourself and other relatives. Draw a picture of a tree and put the youngest generation (children) at the bottom of the tree and the oldest generation (grandparents, great-grandparents) at the top of the tree, as shown. Draw lines to link people together.

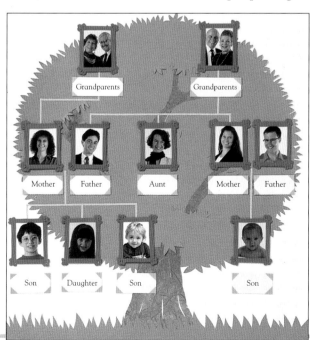

Plan out the whole tree before you stick down the photos.

Write names, birth dates, and death dates beneath each picture.

If you don't have any photographs, just write in the person's details.

Time capsule

Make a collection of small objects that show what life is like today, such as a diary of a week in your life, photographs, newspaper cuttings, stamps, and a shopping bill. Put them inside an airtight jar and bury it for people of the future to find.

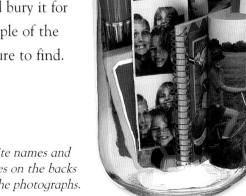

Write names and dates on the backs of the photographs.

Find out as much as you can about a famous person who lived in your town.

Under the Sun

Everyone knows that the Sun keeps us warm and helps plants to **grow**, but did you know that the Sun can do many other things too? There's more to the **Sun** than meets the eye!

Which way?

If you are lost and the Sun is out, you can use your watch to find your way. In the northern hemisphere, point the hour hand at the Sun. South is midway between the hour hand and 12 o'clock. In the southern hemisphere, point the 12 o'clock position at the Sun. North lies midway between 12 and the hour hand.

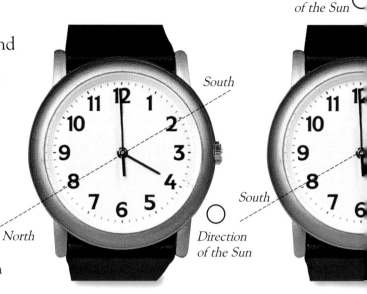

Direction of the Sun

South

North

Direction of the Sun

South

Use this diagram in the Northern hemisphere.

Use this diagram in the Southern hemisphere.

What's the time?

Did you know that you can use the shadows cast by the Sun to tell the time? It's easy! Make this simple shadow clock, or sundial, and put it into your garden. Whenever it is sunny, you won't need a watch to tell the time – just look at your sundial!

You will need

- Large sheet of yellow card
- Orange, red, and white card
- Glue
- Long piece of dowelling
- Flowerpot
- Modelling clay
- Acrylic paints

1 Draw a large sun shape with lots of rays on to a piece of yellow card. Cut it out carefully. Then cut out some red and orange triangles and glue around the edge as decoration.

2 Glue a circle of card to the back of your sun to strengthen it. Carefully make a small hole in the centre of the sun shape, then push a long piece of dowelling through it.

3 Push the dowelling through the hole in the bottom of the flowerpot and secure in place with modelling clay. Decorate the flowerpot with brightly coloured acrylic paints.

Did you know that green **plants** use the Sun's **energy** to make the oxygen we need to live?

Into the light

Try this interesting experiment with a bean. Cut out a hole in the top of a box and add short platforms of card inside, as shown. Plant a bean in a pot of compost and place it in the box. Ensure that no light can enter the box except by the hole. Water it, examine it every day, and watch what happens!

North

The length of the shadow cast by the stick will vary according to how high the Sun is in the sky.

4 Place your sundial in a sunny spot. On the hour, draw in the position of the stick's shadow and label it with the time. Repeat every hour, until you've drawn in as many hour lines as you can. Your sundial is now ready for use!

And there's more . . .

Sunset scene

Watch a sunset and use the bright colours you see to paint a beautiful evening scene.

Sunlight pictures

Use the powerful force of sunlight to make pictures! Put a sheet of black paper in a sunny place, such as on a windowsill, and place cut-out shapes on top of it. For example, you could make moon, stars, and planet cut-outs. Leave for a week or more before removing the shapes and revealing your sunburnt picture.

Stunning stencils

Cut out a stencil of a sun from a piece of card and use yellow, orange, and red paints to create stunning decorations.

Shadow play

Try making this clever shadow theatre. Cut characters, such as animals, out of card and tape each of them to a thin stick. Shine a light on the characters so that their shadows fall on a wall. Write a story and act it out for your family and friends.

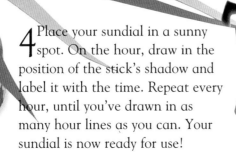

 Did you know that the Sun is around 150 million kms from the Earth?

Making gifts

Home-made presents are extra special. Make these gifts and see how **delighted** your friends and family are to receive them.

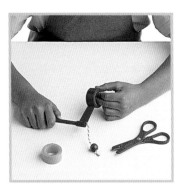

1 Thread a bead onto a piece of cord and tie a knot in one end. Tape the cord to the pointed end of a pencil. Use plenty of tape to make the pencil end wider than the flowerpot hole.

2 Decorate the flowerpot and pencil. Push the pencil through the hole in the pot. Wind elastic bands around the pencil and push them down until the pencil is held firmly in place.

Flowerpot handbell

This unusual handbell is a lovely present to give to a friend and will make a nice decoration for their room.

You will need
- Bead
- Cord
- Pencil
- Sticky tape
- Flowerpot
- Acrylic paint
- Elastic bands

The bead should hit the inside of the rim.

Cool calendar

A calendar is very useful for anyone who can't remember dates! Make a page for each month, tying them on with string. On the left side of the card, stick on pictures cut from magazines. On the right side, write in the month and dates.

Hold a sheet of card lengthways. Mark a line 2 cm from one end, then divide the rest of the card into three sections. Fold at the second line and punch two holes. Fold into a triangle shape and glue the small end flap to the base.

JANUARY

Mon Tues Wed Thurs Fri Sat Sun
1   2   3   4   5   6   7
8   9   10 11   12 13 14
15 16   17 18   19 20 21
22 23   24 25   26 27 28
29 30   31

Potty presents

Decorate a small flowerpot with brightly coloured acrylic paints. Plant a cactus in it and give it to a friend, but don't try to wrap it!

☀ **Flowers** from your garden make a wonderful **fragrant** gift for someone who is housebound.

Truffle treats

These delicious truffles will make the perfect present for a friend with a sweet tooth!

You will need

For the truffles
- 115 g butter
- 225 g digestive biscuits
- 405 g condensed milk
- 4 tablespoons cocoa powder

For the coating
- Vermicelli
- Chopped nuts
- Cocoa powder
- Dessicated coconut

Create your own truffle coatings too.

1 First melt the butter over a low heat. Remove from the heat and allow to cool slightly. Crush the biscuits into crumbs and add to the mixture with the condensed milk and cocoa powder.

2 Spoon the mixture into a buttered, shallow tin, and smooth out the top to level it. Leave it in the fridge to set, then cut into small squares and roll each into a small ball.

3 Put each coating on a separate plate. Divide up the truffles, then roll each group in a different coating. Make your truffles look extra special by displaying them on a plate cut from gold card.

Put your truffles in paper cases to stop them sticking to one another.

Treasure-trove

Make this pirate's chest and fill it with goodies – definitely a gift for someone to treasure!

You will need
- Box with lid
- White card
- Sticky tape
- Glue mixture: 2 parts PVA glue, 1 part water
- Newspaper
- Cardboard
- String
- White paper
- Gold paint
- Coloured beads

3 Next cover the box and lid in strips of white paper that have been dipped in the glue mixture. When dry, paint the box and then stick on the coloured beads.

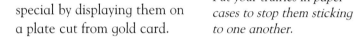
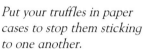

1 To make the domed lid, cut out a piece of card the same length as the box lid but twice as wide. Tape to the lid. Next tape semi-circles of card to each end of the lid, as shown.

2 Cover the box with strips of newspaper that have been soaked in the glue mixture. When dry, decorate the box with shapes cut from cardboard and add details with pieces of string.

 Make a gift **bag** full of **goodies**, jokes, and **puzzles**.

77

Super senses

We use our senses constantly to explore the world around us – what it **feels** like, **looks** like, **smells** like, **sounds** like, even what it **tastes** like. Enjoy exploring these sensational ideas!

Perfect potpourri

Make potpourri to fill the air with fragrant aromas. Finely peel the rind of an orange and a lemon and leave to dry out for 24 hours. Mix with the rest of the ingredients and pour into a jar. Shake the jar every day for eight weeks before opening it and placing it in a bowl.

You will need

- Orange and lemon rind
- 30 g allspice berries
- 15 g whole cloves
- 1 spoon of nutmeg
- 55 g star anise
- 1 spoon ground cloves
- 1 spoon ground cinnamon
- Cinnamon sticks
- Small pine cones
- Sprigs of pine

It's an illusion!

Seeing is believing . . . or is it? Sometimes our brain can be confused by what we see. Straight lines seem to bend, or lines which are the same width appear differently. These are called optical illusions.

1 Using a ruler, draw a series of thick red lines, evenly spaced, on a piece of card. Cut the card into strips, going across the direction of the lines.

2 Place the strips so that every other one is moved slightly to the left. Are the lines straight? Or do they look as if they have become either narrower or wider?

Touch test

How good is your sense of touch? Can you identify objects by their feel alone? Put your friends to the test. Use a box with a hole in the centre as a screen. Your friends must put their hands through the hole to feel the objects. Try to find things that feel unusual. A lot of foods have great textures – try cooked spaghetti, a peeled grape, or a pineapple.

Touching objects when you don't know what they are and you can't see them can be scary!

☀ Ask a friend to shut their eyes. Let them smell an **onion**, but bite into an **apple**. Are they confused?

Sound alert!

Where did that noise come from? Because you have two ears, your brain can work out which direction noise comes from very accurately, but what happens when one ear hears what the other one should? Take two tubes, attach a funnel to the end of each one, then tape them to a piece of wood, as shown. Put some fabric over the tube ends and hold them close to your ears. Listen hard. Is your hearing all mixed up?

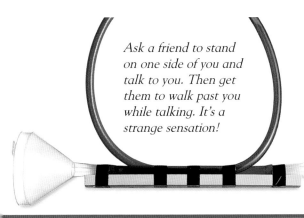

Ask a friend to stand on one side of you and talk to you. Then get them to walk past you while talking. It's a strange sensation!

Tickle those tastebuds

Are your tastebuds up to this challenge? Set up a selection of foods, such as sugar, coffee, salt, vinegar, or milk. Ask a friend to hold their nose and close their eyes while you feed them a little of each substance. Can they identify them correctly? It's more difficult than you think!

And there's more . . .

Dot, dot, dot

People who are blind use a system called Braille to read. Each word is represented by a pattern of raised dots, which the reader feels and interprets with their fingertips. See what you can find out about the Braille system and how it works.

Quick off the mark

Cut a strip of card the same shape as a ruler, divide it into six rectangles, and colour each one. Stick the card to a ruler and hold it vertically. Ask a friend to hold their thumb and forefinger 1 cm apart just below the ruler. Tell your friend they must catch the ruler when you drop it. Without warning, let go of the ruler. Measure your friend's reaction time by seeing what colour they grab. Now swap roles and see how your reaction compares with your friend's.

Hot and cold test

Fill one glass with hot water, one glass with ice-cold water, and the third glass with warm water. Hold one finger in the hot water and another in the cold water for a minute. Now plunge them both into the warm water. What do they feel like now?

The difference will surprise you!

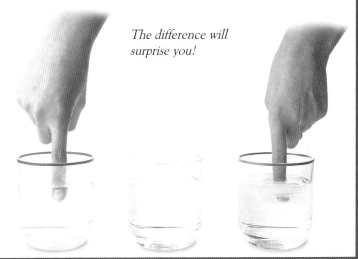

💡 Pour ten **smelly** substances into bottles and **find out** which are your friends' favourites.

Outdoor art

The **best** thing about being outdoors is that you can be really **messy**. When the weather is fine, get **outside**, think **big,** and really let yourself go!

Paint it BIG

Take the largest piece of cardboard or paper that you can find and go to a part of the garden where you are allowed to make a mess! You will need a variety of water-based paints in different colours and a selection of painting tools, such as brushes, rollers, and sponges. Mix the paint with varying amounts of PVA glue if you want to make it thicker.

What will you paint? A space scene? An underwater scene? Or what about an abstract picture of shapes and colours?

Dab paint on with a sponge.

You could even use your hands or feet to apply paint.

Arty gardens

Create a unique work of art that will change in appearance as it grows! Plant straight into the ground, or use a container with a layer of small stones in the bottom, topped with compost. Plant a variety of flowers or herbs, making shapes and patterns as you go. Why not try planting them in the shape of someone's initials?

This herb garden contains parsley, rosemary, golden feverfew, purple sage, and lemon thyme.

☀ Create exciting **sculptures** out of **sand,** dampened with water.

Use a paintbrush to flick paint across the picture.

Experiment with various objects to make patterns in the paint.

Make broad sweeps of paint with a roller.

Junk art

Make an amazing wind chime with old kitchen utensils and cardboard shapes covered in kitchen foil. Construct the framework from twigs, dowelling, or pipe, tying your objects on with string. Watch it catch the light as it chimes in the wind!

A totem pole makes an unusual but attractive garden decoration.

Driftwood designs

When you visit the beach, gather any bits and pieces that would make a great picture. Look out for wood, shells, stones, seaweed, and feathers. Create a face like this one, and try other designs too – just let your mind drift!

Don't pick anything up that might be sharp, like glass or rusty metal.

Totally totem

To make this fantastic totem pole all you need are two pieces of wood and some brightly coloured paints.

! With help from an adult, carefully nail or screw the pieces of wood together, as shown. Draw various designs on the pole, such as animals, birds, or trees, and then paint them. Ask an adult to help you embed the pole in the ground where everyone can admire it.

Use large **stones** and **sticks** to build a 3-D monument.

Out of this world

Is space just full of stars, or is there alien life in another far-away galaxy? Venture into the unknown and find out about our mysterious universe.

Moon diary

Have you ever noticed that the moon looks a slightly different shape each night? Keep a diary, charting the shape of the moon every night for a month. Try and draw the moon at the same time each evening and you will be able to build up a picture of all the phases of the moon.

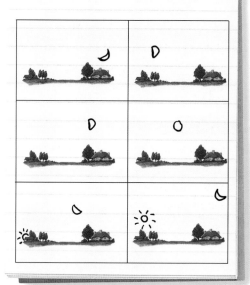

In an alien land

Is there anyone out there? Do you believe that there are planets far away where aliens live? What would such a planet look like? Let your imagination go wild! Make an out-of-this-world alien landscape, add a few weird-shaped aliens, and complete with a high-tech spaceship.

The landscape

1 Create a landscape in the base of a cardboard box. Tape down scrunched-up balls of newspaper to form hills and bumpy land, then cover all of it with layers of kitchen paper. Brush it with the glue mixture, then leave to dry. Paint the surface with the sandy paint.

You will need
- Glue mixture: 2 parts PVA glue, 1 part water
- Sticky tape
- Paint

For the landscape
- Cardboard box
- Newspaper
- Kitchen paper
- Paint with added sand

For the spaceship
- 2 paper plates
- Ping pong ball
- Yoghurt pot
- 4 bendy straws
- 4 pipe-cleaners

For the aliens
- Shuttlecocks
- Tissue paper
- Pipe-cleaners

Stargazer

Stargazing is a great thing to do on a clear, dark night. Wearing plenty of clothes to keep you warm, step outside and take a trip into the strange world of our universe. Find out what different constellations look like, spot them, and chart them noting the time and date. Can you see the Pole Star or the Southern Cross? Try spotting a shooting star or a satellite.

Night-light

Our eyes take time to adjust to darkness. A good tip for drawing at night is to use a red light. So, when you want to write notes, make sure you cover the lens of your torch with red cellophane.

Polaris (The Pole Star)

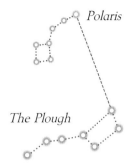

Polaris

The Plough

This star is visible throughout the Northern Hemisphere.

Crux (The Southern Cross)

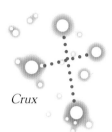

Crux

This constellation can only be seen from the Southern Hemisphere.

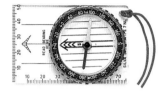

Use your compass to draw the compass points, North, South, East, and West, at the top of your page.

 ! *Always go stargazing with an adult.*

The spaceship

2 Make this spaceship by sticking together two paper plates, front to front. Tape half a ping-pong ball to a yoghurt pot for the ship's top half. Make the legs from bendy straws with pipe-cleaners inside for strength. Decorate.

The alien

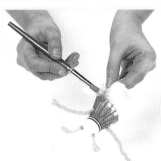

3 Push lengths of pipe-cleaner through a shuttlecock to make alien arms and alien antennae. Soak tissue paper in the glue mixture, roll into balls, and add to the antennae as eyes. Paint in bright, alien-looking colours.

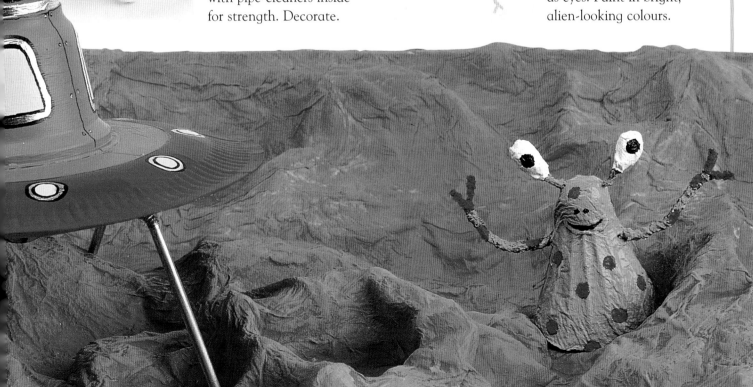

Wheely good fun

Imagine life without the **wheel!** The invention of it certainly made life much simpler. We can **move** around quicker and **travel** over longer distances. Have **fun** with wheels!

Ready, steady, go!

Who is the best cyclist amongst your friends? Create an obstacle course to test and improve your cycling skills – and have fun building it as well.

START

1 Use a stopwatch to time each cyclist. First cycle in and out of a zigzag line of cones, spaced about 2 m apart.

Make start and finish poles with garden canes in paper cones and add paper flags.

2 Build a narrow track with some flowerpots and garden canes. Keep it about 1 m wide. Watch your back wheel around those bends! As you get better, make the track narrower.

Whizz wheels

This recipe will have you and your friends going round in circles – looking for more scrumptious shortbread, that is! Make these finger-licking, lip-smacking wheels in just under half an hour. Remember to set the oven to 180°C/350°F/Gas Mark 4.

You will need

For plain shortbread
- 175 g sieved flour
- 125 g sugar
- 125 g butter
- 1 teaspoon of milk

For chocolate shortbread
- 160 g sieved flour
- 15 g cocoa power
- 125 g sugar
- 125 g butter
- 1 teaspoon of milk

1 To make the plain shortbread, mix the flour and sugar together in a bowl. Cut the butter up into small pieces and rub into the mixture until it looks like breadcrumbs.

2 Make the chocolate version in a separate bowl. Mix as before, but add cocoa powder to the flour. Add a teaspoon of milk to both bowls and mix together to form dough.

3 Divide each batch of dough into three. Make six 15-cm squares and brush them with milk. Place the chocolate squares on top of the plain ones. Roll them up and cut them into slices.

? Did you know that wheels were first used for transport over **5,000** years ago.

4 Jump on to your bike again and cycle to the finishing line. Duck under the limbo bar, made with a garden cane. It's a good job you're wearing that hard helmet!

FINISH

3 Place two logs about 2 m apart. Carry your bike over them as quickly as possible. If the wheels touch the ground, start again.

If a cane falls, add an agreed amount of seconds to your finishing time, as a penalty.

Cycle polo

Set up a course of six upturned flowerpots in a zigzag pattern. Take a baton and a soft ball and weave in and out of the flowerpots, hitting the ball as you go. You will need to have excellent balance for this challenge and be able to steer the bike with one hand! How fast can you go?

To make a baton, roll up six sheets of newspaper lengthways and secure with strips of tape.

4 Place the slices on a greased baking tray and bake near the top of the oven for 15–20 minutes. When cooked, the biscuits will be a pale, golden colour. Leave them on a wire rack to cool.

And there's more . . .

Wheels, wheels everywhere!

There are wheels on cars, bicycles, and also inside clocks and machines. How many wheels can you find at home?

Wooden cart

Make this cart for a young friend, so they can wheel their toys around in style! **!** Ask an adult to help with any cutting and drilling. Four slices of wood from a branch, with a hole drilled through the centre of each, make great wheels. Attach the wheels to two sticks, then secure with metal staples to a flat piece of wood, making sure the axles can turn. Drill a hole at one end of the cart and attach a string handle.

Learn how to repair a punctucture in the wheel of a bicycle and always carry a puncture repair kit!

Puzzle it out

Everyone enjoys tackling a good puzzle or watching a baffling magic trick. Entertain your family and friends with this brilliant selection of brain-teasers and illusions.

You will need
- Coffee jar lid or similar
- White card
- Felt pens
- Ball bearings
- Cling wrap
- Sticky tape

Rollerball

This is a very simple puzzle to make, but it will keep people occupied for hours. The aim is to get one ball bearing to rest in each of the holes. Give this one to a young friend and make a more difficult version, with more holes and ball bearings, for an adult.

1 Trace around the lid on a piece of card. Cut out the circle and draw a picture on it. Make three holes in it using a hole punch.

2 Colour your picture and push it firmly into the bottom of the lid. Now place three ball bearings on top of the picture.

3 Cover the top with a piece of cling wrap. Make sure it is pulled tight, then tape around the side of the lid with sticky tape.

How did you do that?

This trick involves distracting the audience's attention from what is really happening, so make sure no-one is sitting beside or behind you.

You will need
- Coin
- Plastic cup
- Piece of paper – larger than the cup
- Home-made wand

4 Rest your hand on the table and let the cup fall into your lap. Be careful not to let anyone see this. The paper should keep the shape of the cup.

1 Tell the audience that you are going to make a coin pass through the table. Place the paper over the cup and then place the cup over the coin.

2 Scrunch the paper around the base of the cup. Now, tap the cup with the wand, say a few magic words, and announce that the coin has disappeared.

3 Lift the cup and point to the coin saying, "Oh, it's come back! I'll make it disappear again!" At the same time, move the cup to the edge of the table.

5 Hold the paper carefully, so the people think the cup is still inside. Cover the coin again. As you wave your wand, accidentally slip and squash the paper flat.

☆ Slice a banana without peeling it! Sew thread around it through the skin, then pull the thread ends!

And there's more . . .

Magic loops

Take a long, thin strip of paper. Twist it once and stick the ends together. With scissors, carefully cut along the centre of the paper. Wow! Are you surprised by what happens? Do the same thing again, but twist the paper twice before you glue the ends. Cut as before. What happens this time?

Super balloon

Can you stick a kebab skewer into a balloon without it bursting?! The secret is to place a piece of sticky tape on the balloon before you stick the skewer in. You'll need tape on the other side too. Impress your friends by sticking the skewer right through!

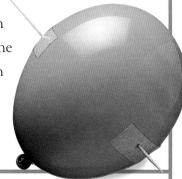

6 Look puzzled. Then lift the paper to reveal the coin. Pretend to be confused. You wanted the coin to disappear, not the cup! Your audience will be surprised, as they expected one thing to happen, and then something else happened instead. Lift the cup from under the table and confess that you need more practice!

Changing shapes

Photocopy the tangram puzzle below. You can enlarge it if you want. Following the lines, cut it into five pieces. Now, can you make the other shapes which are shown? You have to use all five pieces each time. What other shapes can you make?

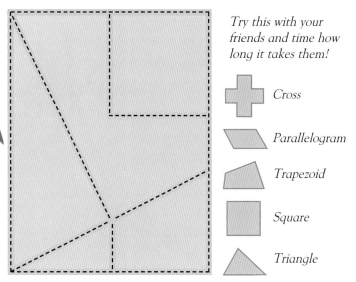

Try this with your friends and time how long it takes them!

Cross

Parallelogram

Trapezoid

Square

Triangle

Camping

Don't just sit around the house – get up and get **out**!
There's lots to see and enjoy when you go camping. So be well
prepared and you'll have a great time. Set your **tent**
up in the garden and invite a friend to **camp** with you.

The great outdoors

Camping in the "great outdoors" can be fun,
whether it's fine or raining. Make sure your
tent is fully waterproof for those unexpected
downpours! Take a good waterproof
groundsheet, a warm sleeping bag,
and a few changes of
clothes. Pack spare
clothes inside a
plastic bag.
Oh, and bring
lots of food too!

! *Always make sure
that an adult is
with you when you
go camping.*

Around the campfire

Sitting around the campfire at night is one
of the best parts of camping. After
your meal, gather around the fire
and toast marshmallows on the
end of a stick. They're very gooey,
but delicious! Tell ghost stories in the
dark and get a friend to hoot like
an owl when you get to a scary part.
The others will jump a mile!

! *Do not attempt to make a
fire. Ask an adult to make
it. Have some water nearby
to put the fire out.*

First-aid

When you are camping, accidents may happen,
so be prepared. Put together a good first-aid
kit and make sure you know how to use it.

• For a graze or a small cut, wash and dry the
wound. Apply antiseptic cream and a plaster.
• A thorn or a splinter in the skin can be
removed with a pair of tweezers. Wash and dry
the area afterwards and put on antiseptic
cream and a plaster if necessary.
• If there is a serious accident, call
the emergency services and find
an adult immediately.

⚡ **Invent** a story! Each person has a minute to tell a **story**, before the next person continues the tale.

Turn the skewers regularly so the kebabs cook evenly.

Barbecue food

A barbecue is a great way of cooking outdoors. The food always tastes really good and it's much more fun than cooking indoors! Prepare some kebabs by threading small sausages, chopped peppers, courgettes, and onions on to a skewer. Cook the kebabs on the barbecue, while the potatoes, wrapped in foil, cook in the charcoal. **!**

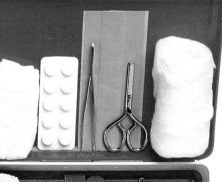

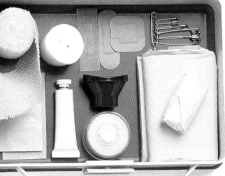

A first-aid kit should include:

- Antiseptic cream
- Antiseptic wipes
- Sling
- Crepe bandage
- Sterile gauze
- Plasters
- Padded dressing
- Scissors
- Tweezers
- Safety pins

Trail-finders

Laying a trail or tracking one that someone else has set, is a great way to spend the afternoon. First, you will need to agree a set of signs like the ones shown below, using twigs, stones, or leaves. Make a record of your signs and their meanings in a notebook for future use.

"Not this way." Place at a point where the tracker may take a wrong turn.

"Walk four paces." The tracker should count out four paces to the next sign.

"Go home." The tracker has reached the end of the trail and should return to base.

Get the permission of an adult before you go out and tell them where you are going.

It's more fun to set the trail in pairs, so find three friends to track with. Give the pair laying the trail a ten-minute start before following with a friend. The signs should be set on the same side of the path and not too far apart.

-💡- Listen! How many different **birds** can you hear singing in the dawn chorus?

On the ball

There are lots of **games** to play with balls: football, cricket, tennis. Here are some alternatives that you'll enjoy making as much as you'll enjoy **playing** them.

You will need

- Pair of tights
- 250 g of lentils
- Thread
- 2 wooden curtain rings
- Strong glue
- 2-m pole
- Coloured tape
- 1.5 m of cord

Swing ball

If you play ball games outside, and spend more time retrieving the ball than you do playing with it, you'll love this game – because the ball can't get away!

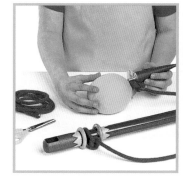

1 Cut the pair of tights in half. Pour the lentils into one toe and twist the end. Wrap the material back over the ball and tie with thread.

2 Glue the two wooden rings near the top of the pole, as shown, leaving a 5 cm gap between them. Decorate the pole with tape.

3 Tie one end of the cord to the "lentil" ball. Tie the other end to the decorated pole, between the two curtain rings.

4 Push the pole into the ground. The two players stand opposite each other with the pole between them. Taking it in turns, one hits the ball clockwise, the other anticlockwise. The first to wrap the ball around the pole scores a point.

Set a target score. The winner could be the first person to reach ten points.

Dodge ball: Players **dodge** soft balls thrown by two others. Anyone hit below the knee is out.

Papier mâché ball

This papier mâché ball filled with goodies would make an excellent present for a friend. Or you can use it to play this smashing game!

You will need

- Balloon
- White paper
- Glue mixture: 2 parts PVA glue, 1 part water
- Sweets
- Sticky tape
- Paint
- String
- Length of dowelling
- Coloured tape

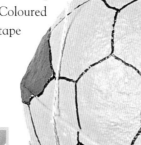

1 Cover a balloon with pieces of white paper soaked in the glue mixture. Cover in several layers of paper and leave to dry.

2 Cut the paper shell in half and remove the balloon. Put some sweets into the shell and tape it together securely.

3 When dry, decorate the ball and hang it up with string. Now each person takes it in turn to strike the ball with a piece of dowelling while blindfolded. The hitter can keep any sweets that fall out during their turn.

Decorate the dowelling with strips of coloured sticky tape.

Blow football

You'll need a lot of puff for this game of football. Use bendy straws to blow the ping-pong ball across the pitch and into your opponent's goal.

You will need

For the goals
- Netting fruit bag
- Bendy straws
- Sticky tape
- Modelling clay

For the pitch
- Cardboard box
- Green card
- White chalk or paint
- Paint

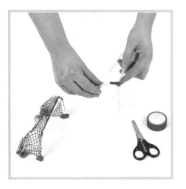

1 To make the goal frames, cut lengths of bendy straws and tape them together. Make the nets with the netting from an orange bag and tape to the straws.

2 Mark a football pitch with chalk on a piece of green card and place it inside the box which has been cut as shown. Decorate the stands with supporters. Secure the goals to the pitch with modelling clay.

Hands up!

You'd be amazed at all the great things you can do with your **hands** – make cards **disappear** into thin air, bring **socks** to **life**, create great works of **art**, and record fingerprints!

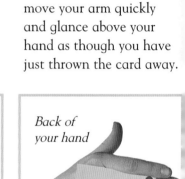

Make the card disappear . . .

To perform a sleight-of-hand trick you need to make quick hand movements that no-one else notices. This takes hours of practising, but is worthwhile when you see an audience amazed by your skill.

Now you see it!
Stand side-on to your audience. Show them the card held between your fingers and thumb. Now follow the steps below.

Now you don't!
As you perform steps 1–4, move your arm quickly and glance above your hand as though you have just thrown the card away.

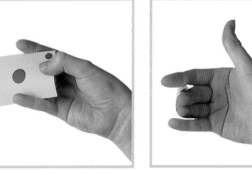

Back of your hand

1 Lower your arm slightly and bend your second and third fingers behind the card. Hold your first and little fingers at the side of the card as shown.

2 Trap the card between your first and little fingers, with the second and third fingers bent. If you find this hard, don't give up. It will come with practice.

3 Straighten your second and third fingers. Do this quickly and the card will flip to the back of your hand. Don't worry if it falls the first few times you try this.

4 Raise your arm slightly and straighten all your fingers. The card stays trapped between your first and little fingers, but the audience can't see it.

. . . and reappear!

The people watching will be amazed so far, but they will be astounded when you bring the card back again!

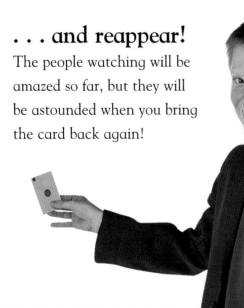

1 To bring the card back, bend your fingers. Do this quickly while moving your hand forward, as if you are catching the card in mid-air.

2 Free the card from your little finger. Turn it so the audience can see it held between your first finger and thumb. Soak up the applause

Sock puppets

These sock puppets are very easy to make, but be sure to use clean socks! The eyes and noses are made of buttons. You can even add hair by sewing on bits of wool.

Scissors, paper, stone

This is a great game for two players. You can play it anywhere you like, in the car, on an aeroplane, or even on the beach! All you need is your hands! Players sit opposite each other. Each clenches a fist and chants "Jan, Ken, Pon." On the word "Pon", both players display their hand in one of these three positions.

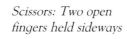

Scissors: Two open fingers held sideways

Paper: A flat hand held sideways

Stone: A clenched fist

Scoring

Stone and scissors:
Stone blunts scissors, so stone wins.

Paper and stone:
Paper wraps stone, so paper wins.

Paper and scissors:
Scissors cut paper, so scissors win.

The same symbols:
If you both make the same hand symbol, it is a draw.

Fingerprints

If you fancy yourself as a detective, you will need to practise taking fingerprints. Ask friends and family to be your suspects. See pages 60–61 for how to find fingerprints at a crime scene.

1 Take a sheet of paper for each person and draw two rows of five boxes. Write the person's name at the top of the paper.

2 Using an ink pad, ink the suspect's thumbs fingers and press them on to the paper, one fingerprint per box. Use a separate row for each hand.

And there's more . . .

Hand-printing

Sponge paint onto the palm of your hand and make a print on paper. Use different colours of paint and other parts of your hand to create a picture.

Finger puppets

Cut two pieces of felt, one for the back and one for the front. Sew together around the edge, leaving an opening for the finger! Add features with small pieces of felt.

Index

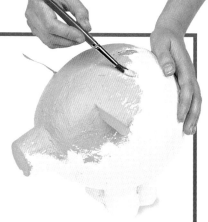

Acknowledgments

Dorling Kindersley would like to thank the following people for their help in the production of this book: Joe Hoyle for the jacket design; Sue Leonard, Susan Malyan, Selina Wood, and Penelope York for editorial help; Eun-A Goh, Jacqueline Gooden, Robin Hunter, Tass King, Carole Oliver, Jane Tetzlaff, and Martin Wilson for design help; Jim Copley for making models and props; Jane Horne for additonal prop-making; Dorian Davies for additional illustrations; Hilary Bird for the index; Andy Crawford for additional photography; Dorothy and Rosie Levine for modelling; Katie Foster for the footprints. Every effort has been made to trace copyright holders, and we apologize in advance for any unintentional omissions. We will be pleased to insert the appropriate acknowledgment in any subsequent edition of this publication.

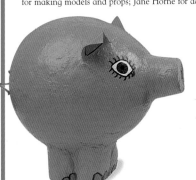
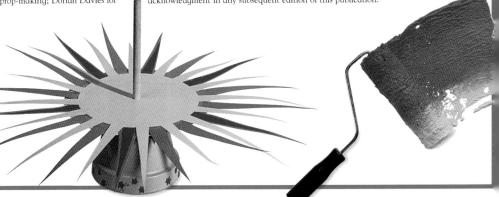